1

'She's only a pup, not that you'd know to look at her,' Barney, a farmer who lived a short distance away from me in the village, said, as we surveyed the black greyhound that was rushing around the ancient yard, chasing a barrel-bodied yellow Labrador.

'She seems very energetic,' I agreed. 'Why are you getting rid of her?'

'I never wanted another dog in the first place.' The old-timer sighed. 'Only took her in 'cause I ran her over, and when no one claimed her, the vet was goin' to put her to sleep. She needs walking and loads of attention. I'm afraid all I'm interested in of an evenin' is sitting in front of the fire with a mug of tea. I'm too old for all that class of high jinks.'

I nodded and watched the mutt, who was now down on her belly, slowly edging her way towards a scruffy thrush that had perched on a sprig of ragwort. I remembered reading somewhere that greyhounds were initially hunting dogs, and here was the evidence – they are hounds, after all.

'Does she have a name?'

'I call her Millie,' Barney said.

'Does she answer to it?'

'When it suits her. She's smart enough in fits and starts.'

'I wish the same could be said of me.'

I got up and went across the broken concrete. Millie completely ignored my approach, still focused on the bird, which was utterly oblivious to her. I crouched down and said, 'Bang.'

The thrush took off in an explosion of feathers and air. Millie jumped up and loped around for half a minute, apparently letting the thrush know that this was her territory and he'd better not forget it, then sat down again, panting heavily. I reached over and ruffled her ears. She was black all over, with some white on her paws and underbelly and a white tip to her tail. I had never seen a greyhound pup before. She was not unlike a black furry snake with four long legs. I scratched her stomach – she rolled over and bared it for me. 'Well, you're a pretty girl, aren't you?' I asked her.

Millie didn't say anything, but I knew she agreed.

Barney sidled over. 'You two gettin' along, then?'

I grinned. 'What does she eat?'

'I'll get you the bag of stuff. Costs a fair whack, but greyhounds have delicate metabolisms.'

'They would.' I sighed.

Millie proved to be just the companion I was looking for. It took a few days to get her settled into the little cottage I rented, and I had a night or two of crying to contend with (I refused to have her in my bedroom when I discovered it would mean sharing my bed with her) but she soon got used to her own blanket on the kitchen floor. And there was so much to see around the small village I had come to call home that we were never short of interesting and challenging walks.

I had been living the rural life for two years. I'd been working in child protection for the Dunleavy Trust, which was dedicated to helping children in crisis, and had fled the city after a series of tough cases. Since then, I'd made my living playing music in pubs and for the occasional folk club. I had also volunteered at the Drumlin (Therapeutic) Training Unit, a daycare centre for adults with intellectual disabilities; in recent months the help I'd been giving had turned into a paying job.

Drumlin was a really special place. I had worked before in settings where 'integration' was the order of the day, but never before had I seen it so powerfully applied. Many of our clients had endured very tough experiences – they'd been forced to live in awful institutions or put up with being ignored or ridiculed by society at large. In Drumlin, everyone was treated with respect and compassion, informed by the belief that each person is valuable and important in their own right.

I had held off making my role at Drumlin official until I'd felt ready to take on the responsibilities of a full team member. After all, I had left the city to avoid the pressures of a job that was taking over my life. But Drumlin was a breath of fresh air. Tristan Fowler, who ran the place, was incredibly experienced and charismatic and had made me feel that my talents and opinions were genuinely needed – although, of course, the place wouldn't fall apart without me.

In truth, my time at Drumlin had been as much about healing my own wounds as it had been about helping anyone else. And it had worked. I now felt that I could be useful. I stopped hiding, and returned to the fray.

When Millie and I got to know one another, Drumlin was on a short summer break. My home was in a tiny hamlet set amid a network of narrow country roads that ran for ten miles in every direction. The nearest town was a twenty-minute drive away. And that was how I liked it.

On a warm sunny afternoon in late July Millie and I, with my friend and colleague from Drumlin Lonnie Whitmore, were having a picnic by one of the many lakes that dot the countryside in that part of Ireland. The locals were very proud of them. I had complained to Lonnie when we first met that navigating the myriad narrow roads of the midlands was nigh on impossible because lakes took priority on sign-posts while towns often didn't warrant a mention. Lonnie, characteristically acerbic, had told me to stop moaning and buy a map. I'd taken his advice.

That day several other groups were gathered here and there about the banks of Ballyfurbo Lake. Some, like us, were stretched out on the grass that spread for half an acre or so in front of the lough and sharing a meal, while others kicked footballs or tossed frisbees to dogs. Millie was acutely aware of the other dogs, standing stock still on point, look-ing purposefully at them, wagging her tail and whining in frustration when they failed to respond to her overtures.

Lonnie, ironically, had quite the other problem: he was receiving the usual stares and comments from almost every-one who went past. We had both become used to ignoring the catcalling and uncomfortable glances. Lonnie was a dwarf, and one who was completely comfortable in his own skin. If people were disturbed by his appearance, then that was their problem, so far as he was concerned.

'Don't you ever just make a few sandwiches?' Lonnie asked, as he picked up a barbecued chicken wing I had packed. There was also home-made ciabatta, a pot of lemon hummus, a salad Niçoise, a flask of coffee and some iced cranberry green tea.

'Are you complaining?' I asked, raising an eyebrow.

'No. This is great. It's just that when you said we were going to have a picnic, I imagined something a little less . . . elaborate.'

'If a task's worth doing . . .'

4

'Yeah, all right, Delia Smith. Pass me some more of that bread.'

When all the food had been either eaten or packed back into the boot of my old Austin, Lonnie and I strolled along the edge of the lake. Millie ranged here and there ahead of us, her nose almost in the water as she scuttled about, startling a mallard or moorhen every now and again.

'I hear there are big changes afoot at work,' Lonnie said.

'How so?'

'You know Tristan's held out against accepting money from the Health Services all these years.'

'I do.' Drumlin had run independently since its inception, based on goodwill and whatever funding it could raise itself. Tristan had grudgingly agreed to take money from the state in the past, but always found that, in return, he was expected to hand over much more control than he was comfortable with or to accept a client who was totally unsuitable for the centre.

'Well, a little bird told me,' Lonnie continued, 'that he's accepted some money from the Church.'

'The *Church*?' I spluttered. 'That makes no sense. I mean, Tristan hates religion. Won't even allow it to be discussed in the unit.'

'I know. But you have to remember, when he had no premises to work out of, the local convent came to his rescue. I think he can make the distinction between the bad things religious orders have done in the past and the good they can do now if they put their minds to it.'

I thought about the implications of this piece of news. 'So how will his accepting a grant or a donation make any difference to you and me?'

'Well, the way I hear it, he's accepting a lot more than just money.'

'Just one minute, Mr Secret Agent,' I said, laughing. 'What do you mean "the way I hear it"? Who's telling you all this stuff?'

'*The way I hear it*,' Lonnie continued, as if I hadn't said a word, 'is that the Sisters of Mercy, from whom he has accepted financial assistance, run several community settings in the area. Tristan will be taking over responsibility for one of them.'

'And what are these centres, exactly? Homes for the elderly? Drop-in centres for teenagers?'

Lonnie shrugged. 'Dunno. We'll just have to wait and see, won't we?'

Millie started barking. For a second, I couldn't see her, or work out where she might be. The lake opened up to our left, reeds poking through the shallows, branches of trees and bushes overhanging it like the fingers of giants. Millie was usually a quiet dog: when she barked, it meant she was either excited or distressed.

'She's over there,' Lonnie said, nodding towards a bank of scrub.

My friend could move remarkably quickly for his size, and I was constantly amazed by how agile he was – he had taken off across the soggy ground, heading towards a bunch of reeds from which Millie's barking seemed to be coming. I followed, assuming she had come across a swan's nest or perhaps an angry bull heron, determined to defend its territory.

I was wrong.

When I rounded the reeds, I found Lonnie standing up to his knees in the water, Millie's collar firmly in his grasp. She was still barking, her whole body trembling, trying to escape from Lonnie. Around five yards out into the water, clinging to a branch that overhung the lake, gazing wordlessly at the man and the noisy dog, was a small child.

I blinked and shook my head. I could hardly believe my eyes. She was probably two or three and seemed to have a head of blond curls, but they were plastered to her skull with water. She was wearing a blue T-shirt.

'What do we do?' Lonnie asked nervily.

The child watched us with huge dark eyes. I waded out into the water a little. I was wearing red Converse high-tops, and the water was seeping through the fabric. 'Hey, honey,' I said. 'Why don't I get you in from there? I think you're a little out of your depth.'

The child made no sound or movement. I sloshed out past Lonnie and Millie. She watched me coming. Just as I got to her, she let go of the branch and disappeared into the dark water.

'Shit!' I plunged my hand into the lake. For a second I couldn't find her and panicked, but then I felt a small, pudgy arm, and hauled the dripping child out. I expected her to take a gulp of air or start crying, terrified after her near-drowning, but she did neither. Instead, she sank her teeth into my arm.

I yanked her loose, but she immediately tried to fasten on to my hand, so I flung the thrashing water-sprite over my shoulder – it would be difficult for her to gain purchase on anything other than my shirt there – and waded back to shore.

'Maybe you should toss her back,' Lonnie said, in a bemused tone, as she fought for freedom.

'I'm considering it,' I muttered.

We'd walked a good distance around the lake, perhaps a kilometre away from where most of the families had been, and by the time we got back, most had packed up and gone. There were one or two little groups still around the wide green area, but if there was any hue and cry about a missing child, it was very quiet. We paused and looked about the expanse of grass, hoping to see someone who appeared to be even slightly alarmed. We were disappointed.

'Only one thing for it,' Lonnie said. 'We'll have to go door to door.'

She belonged to the fourth group we encountered. They hadn't noticed she was missing, and seemed utterly unconcerned that she had almost drowned.

'Um. . . she's just a little upset,' I said, depositing the sodden child on the rug the young couple were sprawled upon. They were probably in their early twenties. She had long, dishwater-blond hair pulled tight back, and wore what looked like a pair of not altogether clean pyjamas and beige imitation Ugg boots; he, sporting a shaved head, was clad in a scuffed leather jacket, a stained white T-shirt and khaki combats. Their picnic appeared to consist of a six-pack of Dutch Gold lager and a supermarket own-brand bottle of vodka. Some empty *fromage frais* tubs showed a modicum of consideration for the child.

'Just leave her there. She's a little fucker for wanderin' off,' the young woman said, her voice noticeably slurred.

'Do you have any dry clothes?' Lonnie asked. 'The heat's already goin' out of the day.'

The woman narrowed her eyes at him, as if she had only just noticed he was there. 'Are you a gnome or somethin'?' she asked, pronouncing the *g*. I sighed inwardly.

'I'm more of a goblin,' my friend said, deadpan. 'We love the water, you see. Gnomes only live around woods and in gardens.'

'Really?' the woman said, seemingly fascinated.

'Oh, yeah,' Lonnie continued. 'You got any way to bring the little one home?'

'I have me van,' the man said, gesturing towards a rusted Hiace some twenty yards away.

The child was eyeing the adults, edging off the mat, her focus the nearby reeds. I angled myself to intercept an escape attempt. 'And do you think you're okay to drive?' I asked. 'Looks like you put away quite a bit of booze there.'

It was the man's turn to bristle. 'I don't reckon that's any o' your business.'

I shrugged. He was right, but I wasn't happy to leave the little girl in the state she was in.

'I'll be back in a minute,' I said, and jogged over to the car. I kept a towel in it in case Millie decided to run through puddles. I had just washed it, so it was perfectly clean. I went back to where Lonnie stood, and handed the towel to the man.

'This'll keep her warm until you're ready to leave.'

He took it and reached for another can. The child, whose name I still did not know, took off in the direction of the lake. The woman laughed and made no move to go after her.

'I'll get her.' Lonnie sighed. In two deft movements, he had the little girl under one of his arms.

'You need to keep an eye on her,' I said sharply. 'The lake gets deep very quickly.'

'Yeah yeah. 'Bye now,' the man said.

'Come on,' Lonnie said, and clicked his tongue at Millie – she had lain down and seemingly gone to sleep during the exchange.

I had a last look at them as I turned the Austin onto the road. Through a break in the hedge I saw the man lying flat on his back, the bottle of vodka, in one hand, balanced on his chest. The woman was sitting, her arms wrapped around her knees, my towel draped about her shoulders. The little girl was nowhere to be seen. In the five minutes since we had left them, she had made off again. I decided to put the family out of my head and go home.

2

On our first day back to work after the summer break, Tristan called me into his office. Somehow I knew I was about to learn how accurate (or not) Lonnie's prediction about the future of Drumlin had been.

At nine thirty the clients were scattered about the open-plan workspace, drinking tea and chatting about what they'd got up to on their holidays. I was setting out the chairs for the morning news session – the first daily activity: it gave everyone the chance to say what was going on in their lives. It might involve a discussion of the highlights from the previous evening's episode of *EastEnders*, a debate about the local elections or even a heartfelt venting because someone had been discriminated against or bullied – a common feature of our clients' lives.

I was counting the chairs to make sure I had remembered everyone when Tristan stuck his head round his office door and nodded at me. Satisfied that no one would be left standing, I ambled over to him.

Tristan was a tall, well-built man in his fifties with a shock of grey hair. His office, though small, was immaculately tidy: every picture was precisely hung, every file alphabetically ordered, all pens organised by colour and use. He had been in the army for many years, hence his attention to detail. Now he did not beat about the bush.

'There's been one rather dramatic change at Drumlin since I last saw you.'

'Really?' I said. 'And what might that be?'

'We've acquired a new unit.'

I said nothing. I've sometimes found that keeping my mouth shut serves me best.

Tristan continued: 'I needed some capital – which was nothing unusual in light of my determination to retain our independence. The agency who chose to contribute asked that I – we – take a hand in running a small crèche in the village of Brony. It caters for children with developmental delays and behavioural problems.'

I blinked. 'A crèche? You mean an early-years service?'

'One and the same.'

'Have you – um – have you any experience of running a crèche, Tristan?'

He shook his head. 'My entire career has involved working with adults.'

'So what are your plans?'

He smiled. 'You've done some work with younger children, haven't you?'

My mouth dropped open. 'That was years ago—'

'It'll come back to you,' Tristan cut me off. 'The crèche is in crisis, and needs immediate support. Right up your alley, if I'm not mistaken.'

'What about Beth?' I asked – she was Tristan's second-in-command. 'She'd probably love the opportunity.'

'I need her here. As it is, sending you off for a few months will cause enough of a kerfuffle. If I asked her to go, we'd have a total mutiny on our hands.'

11

I was being manipulated, I decided. 'What's the crisis about?'

'The crèche specializes in children with a variety of disabilities and behavioural problems. Many are referred by the health services due to ongoing problems at home. A couple of very tough cases arrived together and have proved very challenging indeed. The woman who'd been running the place couldn't cope and left, and the two remaining staff, both quite experienced, are struggling. They need someone to take a step back from the situation and work out how to deal with the problems positively.'

'These are all pre-school kids? Two to five, say?'

Tristan wobbled his hand, *comme ci, comme ça.* 'Some are a little older. Children with special needs often start school a year or so later than the norm.'

'Of course.'

My boss looked at me inquisitively. 'What do you think?'

I shrugged. 'Might be interesting.'

'So you'll do it?'

'I'll go over and have a look.'

'Tremendous.'

'But only because I see it as an opportunity to broaden my knowledge of special needs,' I said firmly. 'I haven't worked in a childcare setting in a while and, as I told you when I started here, I don't do trouble-shooting any more.'

'All I ask is that you give the place the once-over and see if you can't help the staff.' Tristan was unable to hide his delight.

'I dare say the staff will be giving me direction, not the other way around.' I sighed.

That was the last occasion on which I was right about anything for a very long time.

3

Brony was around fifteen miles from Drumlin. Tristan had given me directions to the building (a community centre) from which the crèche, Little Scamps – I shuddered at the name – operated and, since I had played music in the village pubs a couple of times, I knew my way around.

I rang the bell.

After a minute or two, a tinny voice said, through a small speaker, 'Yes? Can I help you?'

'I'm Shane Dunphy. From Drumlin Therapeutic Unit?'

The speaker hissed into silence and a buzz told me the door had unlocked. I pushed it and went inside.

The first thing that hit me was the noise. I had forgotten just how overwhelming it could be in a busy crèche, a crescendo of screeches and whoops, scraping furniture and crashing toys. I stood for a moment just inside the door to acclimatize, then went into the main room. It was brightly painted and well resourced, with all the usual play areas – craft, dress-up, the home corner, storytelling, sand-and-water, music. I tried to count the children but soon gave up: they were moving too fast and were often physically entangled with one another. In terms of special needs, I could see two children with Down's syndrome, and one with his legs in braces – he used crutches to propel himself at lightning speed about the room.

A harassed-looking woman approached me from amid the chaos. 'You're the Dunphy fella?'

'Shane Dunphy, yes – pleased to meet you.'

I extended my hand, but she ignored it, calling into the maelstrom: 'Tush, I'm takin' the new lad into the office for a minute or two. Can ye manage?'

I spotted a blond girl, possibly twenty-five or -six, down on her hunkers near the far wall. She waved a hand at her colleague and we moved towards a doorway, which opened on to an office with a large window overlooking the crèche.

The workspace was nowhere near as organized as Tristan's: papers, accounts, files, sandwich wrappers and coffee cups were spread here, there and everywhere.

'Sit if you can find room,' the woman grunted.

I moved a bundle of catalogues advertising play equipment and did as I was instructed.

'Now,' the woman said, finally seeming to relax a bit, 'they've sent you to replace Beatrice.'

'Drumlin Therapeutic Unit has been asked by the Sisters of Mercy to take over Little Scamps,' I said. 'Tristan Fowler, who runs Drumlin, asked me to come and see if I can help. I'm not planning on replacing anyone. I'm here to learn and, hopefully, offer an extra pair of hands. Which it looks like you can use.'

'Oh, we can use twenty pairs of hands,' the woman said, watching the mayhem dispassionately.

'I didn't catch your name,' I said.

'Oh – I'm Susan.'

She was small, but looked strong, and had short dark hair. I guessed her age at late thirties, but she could have been more or less by five years on either side. 'How can I be of assistance?'

She turned her gaze on me, and I saw that she was as close to burn-out as I had ever seen anyone. 'You really want to come and work here?' she asked, clearly incredulous.

'I'd like to try.'

She stood up, beckoning me to join her at the window that looked out over the children.

'Right there is where we need as much help as you can bring,' she said, pointing to the small library corner. 'That little girl . . . that child is where things really started to go wrong.'

At first all I could see was a tousled blond head. Then suddenly the child jumped up and bolted across the room, a heavy picture book held firmly in both hands. She came up at speed behind the little boy on crutches and walloped him hard with it on the back of the head. He went down like a ton of bricks, and suddenly every kid in the place was piling in. I watched the blond waif, who now stood back from the chaos she had caused. It was then that I realized I knew her. It was the little girl from the lake.

'We'd better get out there,' Susan said.

'I think you might be right.'

4

It was six o'clock. The day had passed in a blur. Little Scamps, I thought, was going to be more about containment than anything else. In my six hours in the place I had not learned a single child's name, I had not had one proper conversation with any of the group, and no one had told the kids who I was.

I had broken up fights, put plasters on cuts and grazes, dodged flying projectiles, cleaned up green vomit – a child had consumed a bottle of poster paint – and tried to keep the main passageways free of obstacles. The child with the crutches was nimble but was constantly tumbling over toys.

I sat with Susan and Tush in the now silent crèche and breathed a sigh of relief. 'Ladies, you have my admiration,' I said, raising my mug of tea in a toast. 'This is . . . a very *challenging* job.'

'Are you coming back tomorrow?' Tush asked, clearly expecting my answer to be in the negative.

'If you'll have me.'

Susan laughed. 'Right now, we'd take Ted Bundy so long as he promised to eat Tammy first.'

16

'Tammy is the little blond girl,' I said. 'The one who hit the boy on crutches with the encyclopedia.'

'He's called Ross. You acted as if you knew Tammy. You seemed surprised.'

'I ran into her and her family a fortnight ago. Never thought I'd see her again.' I told them about my experience with Tammy and her parents' apparent lack of interest.

'So you've met Kylie and Dale too, then,' Susan said.

'Yes. I'm not sure what to say about them.'

'That's a common response. They're quite the pair.'

'So what's the problem with Tammy, then?' I asked. 'Has she been diagnosed with any specific disorders? Asperger's? ADHD? Dyspraxia?'

'There are days when she seems to have everything and nothing,' Tush said. 'But then she contradicts what you're convinced is her problem and confounds all expectations. Here's what we do know. She doesn't speak . . . doesn't make any sound at all, in fact. She has some kind of social disability – she seems incapable of forming relationships of any sort – and is excessively violent. She responds to anything that upsets her with aggression. She will not engage in any group activities and prefers to sit on her own. She is a serious flight risk – if we didn't have that security door, she'd be out of here and we'd never catch her.'

'She seems to have good gross motor function,' I said, referring to the major movements people make – walking, jumping, climbing. 'I've seen her run, and she had a very focused swing when she hit Ross with the book.'

'She has fine motor skills, too,' Susan said. 'She uses a knife and fork perfectly, and would you believe that she can tie her own shoelaces?'

I scratched my head. 'So what have we got here? Attachment problems? Neglect? Developmental delays? Genius?'

Susan smiled. 'Any and all of the above.'

'Have you got a plan for her?'

'We've tried plan after plan. They're useless if the child won't engage with anyone. We've tried to get people she knows to help her – even her good-for-nothing mother – and we've tested her with strangers. No dice.'

'So she just does her own thing,' I said.

'Have you got any better ideas?' Tush asked.

'Maybe we could come up with something together,' I said.

The two women looked at each other. 'We've been working with that kid for more than a year now,' Tush said, 'and there hasn't been any change in her.'

'I can see you're both nearly exhausted,' I said. 'It can be unbelievably frustrating to work day-in-day-out with a child who just won't give anything back. I've been there. But one thing I *have* learned is that there are very few situations where things can't change.'

My two new colleagues stared at me as if I had three heads.

'How?' Tush asked.

'How what?'

'How can we change things here?'

'What do you think needs changing?'

The girl laughed, a sort of splutter. 'Everything!'

'Well, let's change that, then!'

5

The children arrived by bus at Little Scamps each day at nine o'clock. On my second day they came in to find the room empty of toys and furniture. Susan, Tush and I were waiting for them amid a collection of paint pots, brushes and rollers.

We were going to spend the rest of the week redecorating, fitting in the usual activities around the work. It was a gamble, and one that had the potential to go badly wrong, but I hoped that by taking some time to make the playroom look better, the children might start to feel proud of it, and thereby respect it. None of them thought anything of taking a chunk out of the plasterwork with a chair leg, or writing on the furniture with felt-tip pens, or even disembowelling a soft toy. Secretly I also hoped that when they saw the transformation progressing before their eyes, they might develop a sense of camaraderie – Little Scamps was sorely lacking in any vestige of community spirit.

When I'd broached the idea, Susan and Tush had been less than enthusiastic. There was, they pointed out, nothing inherently *wrong* with the murals and overall décor: why create a lot of unnecessary problems by replacing them? In theory,

I agreed, but if we were to have a fresh start, we needed to wipe the slate clean, figuratively and literally.

Susan was doubtful. 'Most of the children depend on stability and routine,' she'd said. 'If they walk in here and all the toys and furniture are gone, and we're planning to paint over the pictures on the walls, *and* the usual games and activities are cancelled for the foreseeable future, well, I'm guessing we'll have the Little Scamps version of a nuclear holocaust on our hands!'

'I thought about that when I was hatching my plan,' I said. 'There is indeed a set routine at Little Scamps. And I'm sure the children find it comforting and a stabilizing influence. However, they also go out of their way to transform every session into utter chaos. Would you agree with that, Susan?'

'That's fair,' she said.

'Well, I'm not suggesting we dump the timetable. I *am* saying we need a shake-up. Along with freshening up the paintwork, I think we should start sticking rigidly to the rules. As to the usual activities, well, we can stop for storytime, take a break for music, and maybe we could even divide the group into teams and get some to do standard work while others do painting – the possibilities are pretty much endless . . . We can play it by ear, maybe. But the group has to understand that we're going to see an activity through from beginning to end, regardless of what they throw at us. The day-to-day running of Little Scamps continues, but around it we paint the room.'

The women had looked dubious, but they'd agreed to give it a go.

I had no intention of using the children as some kind of cheap labour force, and I was well aware that pre-schoolers have a concentration span that extends, at most, to forty-five minutes, but on average that will get you through twenty minutes of any game before you need to do something completely different. That time could be cut in half for children with intellectual disabilities. I was also acutely conscious of the health and safety issues involved in getting a group of small children to work with paint.

At the centre of all this lay an important issue: the children had been calling the shots. The adults were there, as far as the children were concerned, to get them food, clean up their mess and provide a space for their uproar. They treated Tush and Susan with the contempt that they reserved for one another and seemed to hold no one in high esteem. A major part of this lesson was about mutual respect. I was going to sell it to the kids as selfishness: won't it be nice for you to have a room you helped paint? By doing nice things for ourselves, we learn to be nice to others.

At any rate, that was the idea.

The children stood just inside the doorway, apparently puzzled by the scene before them. No one moved. As I had suspected, with their familiar environment taken away, the group seemed ill at ease and uncertain how to behave. Past experience with children had taught me that every collective will have one or two leaders to whom the others look for pointers as to what they should do. I wasn't sure if that would apply here – children with intellectual disabilities have varying levels of social skills – but it became obvious very quickly who the alpha dogs in the pack were.

I glanced at Tammy automatically: she was the only child I felt I knew, and the one I wanted to know more about. Yesterday had left me with no real sense of any of the others. I had seen them as a cluster of miniature, faceless troublemakers, so my main impression was still of that odd, silent child. That was about to change – dramatically.

Now that things were quiet for a moment and I had, for a short time, the upper hand, I could look at the children who were temporarily in my care. There were ten, including Tammy and Ross. I knew from the higgledy-piggledy files Susan kept that the two children with Down's syndrome were Jeffrey, a four year old with jet black hair and a barrel-like body, and Julie, aged three, so small and pixie-like that she looked as if a gust of wind might blow her away. There are varying levels of the disorder, but many people with Down's go on to hold down jobs and lead perfectly normal, happy lives. The main problem they face is that employers often refuse to accept them as the capable, articulate souls they are. Down's children develop at a different rate from others, speaking and walking later than their peers. Jeffrey could make fundamental, two-word sentences but Julie was still getting by with grunts, and pointing when she wanted something.

Rufus was five and lived on the local travellers' site. His family had been forced to settle in a small local-authority housing estate due to Ireland's policies on nomadic living, which had made the traditional traveller lifestyle virtually impossible. It was difficult to say if Rufus had intellectual problems, but he was severely neglected and backward in development.

Gilbert was three and came with a bundle of nervous tics and rigidly established routines that suggested he was either autistic or suffered from a severe anxiety disorder. He was a beautiful child – he had a mass of blond curls and huge blue eyes – but was angry and aggressive. Everything frightened him, but while fear sent most children scampering for a safe haven, Gilbert always resorted to fighting, tears streaming down his face, clutching any available implement as a weapon.

Mitzi was six, the oldest in the group. She was sociable

enough when the mood took her – but morbidly, frighten-ingly obese: walking was beginning to pose a problem for her, and her parents, pseudo-intellectuals who, bizarrely, ran a local organic farm-shop, just refused to limit her intake of sweets and fried food. Mitzi would settle herself in one spot in the room and remain there for the rest of the day. She seemed happy to use whatever toys were within easy reach, but was not beyond grabbing another child and forcibly tak-ing from them whichever toy they happened to have about them. Mitzi appeared indolent, but she could move with remarkable speed when she wanted to.

Gus, at five, was the joker. He had been born with mild cerebral palsy and walked with an exaggerated roll of the hip. His balance was poor, and although his arms and hands were unaffected, he found it hard to grasp anything for more than a second or two. Every time I looked at Gus he was tumbling head over heels, dropping a bag of blocks, spilling his juice (usually over one of his friends), breaking a toy or looking for something he had lost. It had been suggested that he also had dyspraxia, often referred to as 'clumsy syndrome', but with the cerebral palsy, it was almost impossible to diagnose accurately. Despite all this, Gus was a good-natured child, and the only one at Little Scamps who seemed happy to be there and to like the other children. He was always smil-ing, even when he had hurt himself. It was impossible not to warm to him – he had a great spirit.

Arga was Polish, the adopted child of two local teachers. With strong Slavic features, she looked around four or five, but we were not sure exactly how old she was. She had been found in a flat complex in Krakow, apparently abandoned by her family. She had been living on whatever she could scavenge from a nearby rubbish dump, and the construction workers who found her seemed to believe that a pack of wild dogs had kept a watchful eye over her. How long she had lived like that was anyone's guess, but she had rallied when she was rescued. She had developed a small vocabulary of Polish words, but had no English at all, even though she had been in Ireland for more than a year. She would tolerate no one but Gilbert, of whom she was very protective. Her adoptive parents were close to despair, and hoped that by spending time in a healthy environment with her peers, she might emerge from the darkness that enveloped her. So far, no such breakthrough had occurred – possibly, I mused, because the environment could hardly be called 'healthy'.

The last member of our motley assembly was Milandra. The daughter of an Irish mother and a Nigerian father, she had hair in tight cornrows and blue eyes. She spoke English, Irish (her mother was a *gaelgoir*) and Yoruba, the language of her father's people. She was solidly built, pretty – and uncontrollable. Susan and Tush had told me her parents doted on her, and while she might have been a little spoiled, it was nothing so great as to explain the terrible rage she harboured against the world and just about everyone in it. She never spoke except to scream, bellowing invective in whichever language she happened to use. She was intellectually able enough to start mainstream school but her behaviour meant this was out of the question. There was no way of knowing what was likely to rub her up the wrong way. Milandra was wholly unpredictable.

So, now we gazed at each other over the rows of paint pots. I could feel the tension radiating behind me as Tush and Susan awaited the children's response. The children exuded their own anxiety – they were not used to surprises. How would they cope with this new development? I was sandwiched between the distress of both sides.

'Good morning, everyone,' I said, as no one else seemed to

be in the mood to begin. 'My name is Shane, and I'm going to be working here for a while.'

Milandra threw me a dirty look, and Mitzi simpered from where she had settled on the linoleum. Other than that I might as well not have been there. I soldiered on.

'Susan, Tush and I thought it might be a good idea, seeing as I'm new and we need to get to know one another, if we did a bit of a project.'

'Whassa project?' Milandra asked sulkily.

'What's your name, sweetie?' I asked.

'Nunna your bus'ness.'

'I told you my name. It's polite for you to tell me yours.'

'You jus' fuck off,' Milandra replied. 'Where all de toys?' This to Susan. 'I wanna play now.'

Susan glanced at me, but I said nothing. 'We'll do some free play later, Milandra. Just now Shane is going to explain how we're going to help with painting and doing the room up. Won't that be fun?'

Milandra let loose a bellow of what I assumed was Yoruba. Susan flinched, but quickly recovered her composure. 'You can shout and rant all you like, Milandra,' she said calmly. 'It won't change anything.'

The little girl hauled herself to her feet and stomped over to the nearest tin of paint. She drew back her leg to deliver a mighty kick. I couldn't help but smile. The top of the tin came to Milandra's waist, and was certainly heavier than she was. It did not move. From the howls and hopping about that followed, it seemed that Milandra's main achievement had been to mash her toes.

There was a resounding silence, punctuated only by Milandra's impassioned roars and curses. Then Tammy, her eyes fixed on me, charged the tin, ramming it with her shoulder. It slid an inch or two across the floor. She stopped dead, then followed up with a kick. I couldn't tell if she'd hurt herself – she remained quiet, biting her lower lip.

Each child in turn had a tilt at the tin. Finally Arga and Gilbert joined forces and, together, started to push with all their might. Susan made to stop them, but I shook my head. The lid of the tin was firmly taped down: knocking the can on its side would not pose a problem.

It took them three great shoves. The can tipped over with a dull thud. Milandra whooped in delight, and Jeffrey shouted something. The children's eyes were turned to us expectantly. I went over to the tin, lifted it up, and returned to Susan and Tush. The children had lapsed back into incredulous silence.

'I've never seen them quite like this,' Tush said. 'I don't like it.'

'They don't know what to do,' I said. 'They're not used to working together, and they're not used to being made to do anything they don't want to. They want to stand up to us, but to do that requires a collective effort. Which is what we want.'

'Well, I suppose that was them working together – sort of,' Susan said. 'But what'll happen next?'

'I have no idea,' I admitted. 'I'm hoping they'll burn themselves out, sooner or later, and we can get some work done.'

'I thought you had a plan,' Susan said.

'I didn't say it was a good one.'

'Or even a finished one,' she added.

Arga and Gilbert overturned the tin again, and the rest of the kids started on the others, rocking them from side to side until they tumbled over. When Gus and Ross had dealt with the last one, the children clustered together, Mitzi sprawled on the floor in the middle of them. All were panting after the exertion and seemed just a little less wound up than they had been.

'Here's what I suggest,' I said, when I was sure the frenzy of paint-tipping was really over. 'Why don't we go into the kitchen and have a snack? We can talk about what we're going to do today. Does that sound like a good idea?'

There was a general round of nods and yeses.

'Okay, then,' I said. 'I baked some banana bread last night.'

We left the paint tins strewn here and there, and trooped into the kitchen.

6

The children sat at the table in the kitchen, sulky and annoyed. We handed round juice and banana bread: I had warmed it in the oven and cut it into fingers. There was also some toast and jam for those who wanted it. When everyone was munching we started 'large circle time', a meeting for everyone at which we would plan the day. I knew from talking to Susan and Tush that such a gathering had not been attempted for a very long time at Little Scamps – keeping the kids away from each other was usually seen as desirable – but this was something we all wanted to change. In most crèches and pre-schools the day was punctuated by large and small circle times to give every child the opportunity to talk about what was going on. What's the point in making a collage unless everyone has a chance to have a look at your work and tell you how good it is? I've seen centres where such moments of appreciation never happen, and children are left with a sense that most jobs are pointless. I didn't want Little Scamps to be one of those units – children have to feel they have a voice, and that when they use it, someone will listen.

That first meeting, though, wasn't really about that. The children I was faced with knew very well they had voices.

The problem was that absolutely nobody could listen to them because there was so much background noise and dangerous activity. I wanted to get the children used to dealing with one another and the staff through a medium other than violence, and food was a good way of doing just that. Most people naturally chat at mealtimes – food makes us sociable, amenable. I hoped that would be the case at Little Scamps.

'Okay,' I said, nursing a mug of coffee. 'Let's talk about what's going to happen today.'

'Why you here?' Ross asked, punching Gilbert, who immediately began to wail.

'Me don' like you,' Rufus chimed in over the resulting ruckus. 'You go 'way.'

'I'm here because you need some extra grown-ups at Little Scamps,' I said, as Tush tried to hush Gilbert. 'If you don't have more staff, the place will have to close. There are laws about how many grown-ups have to be in a crèche with the children – it's called "ratios". If the ratio is wrong, the place is shut down. Would you like that, Rufus?'

He had bright red hair and his nose ran constantly. He eyed me with unconcealed distaste, his mouth full of toast. Then he spat at least half of it at Julie, who started to whinge as she picked gobs from her hair. Rufus was oblivious. He continued, 'You go an' we get somebobby else.'

'We've tried to get several other people to work here,' Tush said gently, moving around to help Julie clean herself up. 'Do you remember Mary, the blond lady who was here three weeks ago?'

'She smelt nice.' Mitzi sighed.

'Well, she stayed for just one morning, and then wouldn't come back,' Susan said.

'M'landra hitted her on the head with my lunchbox,' Gus said, smiling at the memory. 'It maked a pop, so it did.'

'And do you remember Dorotia?' Tush said. 'She was Polish, just like Arga.'

'*Arrrrga,*' the child said. She grabbed Milandra's hair and tugged enthusiastically. Milandra squealed at an alarming pitch – I'd had no idea a human being could make a noise like it. Arga didn't either, it seems, for she let go immediately and gawked at her victim in amazement.

'She was pretty. So pretty,' Mitzi purred, apparently unfazed.

'Yes, she was,' Susan said. 'Do you remember she had that lovely long plait, right down her back?'

'She was a long-haired Polack motherfucker,' Milandra growled, picking up her plastic mug and pouring its contents over Ross's head. He did not flinch – he picked up a slice of toast, spread with butter and jam, and stuck it firmly to his attacker's cornrowed hair.

'Well, why do you think Dorotia stopped coming here after two days?' Tush asked, deciding to ignore this latest assault – Milandra didn't appear too concerned about it.

'Me,' Jeffrey said, raising his hand.

'Go on, Jeff,' Tush said.

He pointed at Julie, who was looking angelic – if that's possible when one is covered with semi-masticated toast.

'What did Julie do, Jeffrey?' I asked.

'Pull – her – hair –' he blurted, just before Gus smacked him in the back of the head with a roll of kitchen towel we had left on the table for the children to wipe their hands. It didn't hurt so much as surprise Jeffrey, but he wailed anyway. Susan tutted at Gus, who hooted with laughter.

'Julie decided that it might be a good idea to use Dorotia's plait as a swing,' Susan said to me. 'That last day, every time the poor girl turned her back, Julie would leap from a table or chair and launch herself at it. I know Julie's tiny, but it must have hurt.'

'We suspect she was put up to it,' Tush said, glaring at Ross, 'but obviously Julie's not talking.'

Julie made a kind of bubbling sound and smiled at me. It was hard to imagine this delicate little creature as anything other than sweet and docile. There was obviously another side to her.

'Then there was Una,' Susan said, rocking the still inconsolable Jeffrey on her knee. 'Lasted an hour. She was a rather . . . um . . . well-endowed lady, and Tammy kept punching her breasts. No warning, she would just run over and wallop her in the boob. Freaked Una out completely.'

'You forgot Ruth,' Tush said. 'The kids kept puking on her.'

'Puking?' I asked, amazed.

'We pukeded on her,' Gus said, mimicking someone being sick.

'I don't know how they did it, but they took turns throwing up all over the girl,' Tush said, shaking her head in disgust. 'By the end of the day she was covered from head to toe. We'd got her one change of clothes but we just didn't have any more for her.'

'So you see,' Susan said to Rufus, 'we've tried lots of people. They decided not to work here because you were all so mean to them. And Shane might still choose not to stay. But you really need to give him a chance.'

'He's precious,' Mitzi cooed. 'Such a precious child.'

'Where our stuff gone?' Ross asked, rolling toast into doughy balls and setting these in a row on the table in front of him. 'Why you gots all them paints?'

'We'd like you to help us paint the room the way you'd like it,' I said.

'Him a painter fella?' Milandra asked.

'Why don't you ask him?' Tush said.

'Hey, hairy boy,' Milandra snapped – and was hit on the forehead by one of Ross's toast balls, which he had flicked with great precision.

'I presume you're talking to me,' I said, trying not to smile.

'Yeah. You. You a painter guy?' Milandra asked, as she rubbed the red spot on her face, eyeing Gus with undisguised venom.

'No,' I admitted. 'I'm pretty damn terrible at painting. But I bet some of you are really good at it.'

'Me good,' Jeffrey said.

'I'm good at painting,' Gilbert said, in a wavery voice. 'Mammy says I'm very good at painting.'

'He hardly ever speaks,' Tush hissed in my ear.

I nodded, but continued talking to the children, who seemed to have declared a brief truce.

'See?' I said. 'I bet all of you could add something beautiful to the room. We could make it really special if we pitched in and did our best.'

There were general murmurs of assent. I held my breath. No one threw a mug or screamed abuse.

'Can we paint now?' Ross asked.

'Well . . . yes, you can,' I said.

And so we began.

7

The rest of the morning passed without any major problems. The first task was to paint over the existing surfaces with a base colour, upon which we planned to make a mural to which we would all contribute. The job did not require any great skill or dexterity – the paint could, quite literally, be thrown on. My intention was to do this as quickly as possible so the kids wouldn't become bored, and we could get on with the far more interesting task of doing the actual pictures and scenes that would make the finished product. I was acutely aware that this could not happen that first day, as the initial coat of paint needed time to dry, and was hoping that the children's destructive side would carry them through – that the pleasure of chucking paint at the wall would sustain their interest. Thankfully, it did. The sheer novelty of it, combined with being allowed to do what would previously have been frowned upon, won the day.

We worked solidly for the first hour, then Tush and I took some of them outside to play. To my surprise, Milandra and Gus chose to stay at their posts with Susan, which we agreed to, on the condition that Susan called us if there were any problems.

Little Scamps had a pleasant enclosed play area behind the main building. There were various pieces of equipment (swings, a see-saw, a climbing frame, a sandpit) and ample room for running and jumping. Tush and I kept a close eye on things, but the children expressed no desire for us to get involved in their activities. This was unusual – children usually crave the attention and approval of adults. There was also little interplay between them – they seemed mainly to entertain themselves. We had to separate a minor altercation, but in the main things were quiet and calm.

Seeing that we were in for an easy ride, I perched my behind on one of the swings and beckoned Tush to join me. It was a beautiful morning, and I enjoyed the feel of the sun on my face. I had been trying to give up smoking, and while I had suffered mercifully few physical withdrawals, I didn't know what to do with my hands during the lulls I would previously have filled by lighting up. The swing offered a convenient substitute.

'How do you think we're doing?' I asked, when she was seated alongside me.

'I'm bowled over,' she said.

Tush was a pretty girl, but seemed to be constantly in a state of nervous exhaustion. I had noticed that she rarely made eye contact when she spoke, and thought that the swing would make conversation easier for her. 'How so?' I asked.

'I can't remember how long it's been since we had a morning like this one,' she said, leaning back to make the swing move. 'It's been so . . . peaceful!'

'I'd love to be able to claim credit for that,' I said, 'but it's purely down to the fact that we dropped two major changes on the gang in one go – me, and the painting.'

'Maybe,' she mused. 'I kind of think they want to change, though. It's like they've been waiting for an opportunity.'

'I know what you mean,' I said. 'My boss, Tristan, always says that a child who is acting out really just wants to know that the adults around him care enough about him to make him stop. I think that's probably true.'

'So maybe we can make these children see that we care,' Tush said, her eyes closed as the swing moved lazily in the mid-morning heat.

'Maybe. It'd be nice to think so.'

'You want to hear a secret?'

I shrugged, even though she couldn't see me. 'Sure.'

'Sometimes I hate working at Little Scamps.'

'So why don't you leave, get another job?'

She sighed a deep sigh, as if the weight of the world was on her shoulders. 'I spent three years getting a degree in early-childhood studies, then another year doing a course in special-needs education. That's four years in college.'

I said nothing. Even I could do those maths.

'What kind of an eejit would I be if I ended up working as a waitress after all that time studying? My parents would kill me.'

'I spent much longer than that in college, Tush, and more than a year playing music in pubs not too long ago when the job started beating me up too much.'

She smiled weakly. 'It does beat you up, doesn't it?'

'Sometimes, yeah. And when that happens, it's okay to take some time out. We have to look after ourselves or we'd get swallowed up, and there'd be nothing of us left.'

That smile again. 'Yes. Sometimes I think I might disappear altogether. It's as if I'm being eaten up, a little bit at a time, and there's nothing I can do to stop it.'

I knew that sensation. Most people who work in social care long term have experienced it. 'It's okay to ask for help, Tush,' I said. 'The very best resource any of us have in this game is our colleagues. Have you talked to anyone about how you're feeling? Susan, maybe?'

She turned and grinned at me. 'I'm talking to you.'

I grinned back. 'Yes, you are.'

I was making a mental note to set up regular staff meetings – several staffing issues required addressing, not least of which was that we needed at least one other person to cope with the children we had – when we heard Susan calling. I could tell by her tone that this was an emergency.

'I'll go,' I said. 'You keep an eye on this bunch.'

When I got inside, everything seemed normal and peaceful enough. The walls were nearly finished (Susan had been going at them vigorously with a roller) and I saw no signs of destruction or damage. Then I spotted Gus and Milandra.

'I only took my eyes off them for a second,' Susan said sheepishly.

'Well, it looks as if that's all it takes,' I said.

They were covered from head to toe in paint. It was like looking at two miniature ghosts.

'Do we have enough white spirit?' Susan asked.

'You'll be pleased to hear that this paint is water-based, so all we need do is stick them in the bath,' I said, trying not to laugh. 'Some of the smaller tins will need spirit, though – we'll need to be a little more careful when we get around to opening them.'

'Gus painted me,' Milandra said. 'I'm a little white girl now.'

'I'm a little white girl too,' Gus chirped.

'Come on,' I said. 'Let's get you cleaned up.' If this was the worst thing we had to cope with that day, we'd have got off lightly.

8

Thankfully, it was.

By the time the bus was pulling up outside, the walls were completely covered with new paint, ready for us to adorn them with murals. Milandra's and Gus's clothes had been washed and dried, and though some of the paint remained in their hair, they were none the worse for it. The rest of the children had been, if not pleasant, then at least not wilfully obstructive. Mitzi had punched Gilbert in the gut; Jeffrey had wet himself; Ross had attempted to use one of his crutches as a pole vault in an attempt to leap over Arga, who was kneeling on the floor, and crashed into her.

But all of those altercations were minor. In fact, I would go so far as to say that they were nothing I wouldn't have expected in a standard crèche or junior class. I wondered if perhaps this was going to be an easy assignment after all.

Experience (and common sense) had made me aware that children do not exist in isolation: every behavioural problem stems from some issue within a family unit or a trauma that had happened far away from the childcare centre. I wanted to look at the children's homes and meet some of the parents. That evening I decided to do the home-time run.

The bus driver, a huge bear of a man named Arnold, seemed to view the children with a mixture of amusement and mild tolerance. Janet and Bea, two housewives, were employed to travel with them. They supplemented their income by doing short runs to and from a number of centres and schools about the county. If they were surprised by my decision to come along for the ride, they didn't show it.

The trip took a little over an hour. Gilbert lived in what could only be described as a mansion. A Rolls-Royce was parked out front beside a Mercedes, which was apparently the family runabout. A young man, whom Arnold informed me was a servant, let the child in. He shut the door without looking at us.

Rufus's house had boarded-up windows and a front garden overgrown with weeds. When the bus stopped outside the gate, a woman who looked as if she had stepped from the pages of a John Steinbeck novel came to the door. I asked Arnold to hang on for a minute, and jumped down after the red-haired tearaway. 'Mrs Ward? I'd just like a quick word.'

The woman froze as if I'd threatened to slap her. 'What?'

Rufus had stopped at the door and was gazing at me, wide eyed.

'My name is Shane. I'm going to be working with Rufus for a while at Little Scamps. I just wanted to introduce myself.'

'He in trouble agin?' the woman asked, apparently not having heard a word I had spoken.

I laughed. 'No, he's not in trouble at all. I'm just doing a quick visit to all the children's homes to introduce myself. I was wondering if perhaps some of the parents might like to get more involved in the crèche. We could use a little help from time to time.'

'I'll tell him to behave better, okay?'

She seemed paralysed with fear. It was as if I was speaking a foreign language to her.

'I'll leave you to your work,' I said. I had had my hand stuck out to shake hers, but she never acknowledged it. I got back on the bus.

'Nice chat?' Arnold asked me drolly.

'If I weren't such an optimist, I'd reckon she thought I was going to murder her,' I said, shaking my head in disbelief.

'Had a hard life, that one,' Arnold said. 'Husband drinks and knocks her about. Kids all wild as mountain goats. Never had more than a couple of pennies to rub together.' He tutted. 'She was a real beauty when she was a girl.'

'Looks sixty now,' I observed.

'I'd say she's forty. Maybe even less,' the driver said. 'Hold on to your arses, ladies and gentlement. Next stop, *chez* Milandra.'

'He means my house,' she announced, to no one in particular.

Milandra was met at the door by her granny, a plump, smiling woman with blue-rinse hair.

'I love her dearly, but she has her mother's heart broke,' the old lady said to me. 'She's as clever as a tack, and she'd buy and sell you, but I'm not jokin', the child has a temper on her that'd scare Jack the Ripper.'

'Well, there are certainly issues,' I agreed. 'But she's still very little. Often it's just about setting some clear boundaries and sticking with them.'

'Ah, sure, I know all that. Haven't I raised five children on me own?'

'No small feat,' I congratulated her.

'Milandra behaves well enough for me – I don't take any messin' – but she runs rings around her mother. Terrorizes her.'

'Why do you think that is?'

'My daughter was always a gentle soul. And I think that children can smell fear.'

Most of the parents chatted with me for a few moments, some obviously a little rattled that a man was now working at the crèche, but in the main I was met with friendliness. Arga's parents agreed to help out when they were free, as did Julie's, but even with these occasional extra hands, I knew I would have to talk to Susan and Tush about more staff. That day's episode with the painted children clearly demonstrated that we couldn't manage much longer with so few of us.

Tammy's house was the last stop. Set amid a tiny housing estate that bordered a salt marsh near the coast, it reeked of poverty and desperation. A low wall, which would have posed no challenge to a determined child, acted as a barrier to the wasteland. I could barely see the ocean in the distance, and the smell of salt and stagnating vegetation hung in the air. A lonely heron stood on one leg in the reeds, a soft wind off the sea ruffling its feathers.

Tammy's house was at the end of the row, tucked into a corner as if it were trying to hide. The little girl shot out of her seat, like a cork from a bottle, hauled the door open and dashed for her home.

'Who usually lets her in?' I asked Bea.

'Watch,' she said.

Tammy lifted a filthy, threadbare mat and produced a key. A grimy plastic chair stood beside the doorstep. She hopped up on to it and, standing on tiptoe, fitted the key into the lock. With great effort and determination she twisted it and, using her foot, pushed the door open.

'I don't fucking believe what I'm seeing,' I said. 'She does this every day?'

'Yep,' Bea said. 'Sometimes her mother sticks her head out after the child goes in, but usually not.'

'So she might well be going into an empty house?' I said.

Janet shook her head. 'The parents are in there. When I started I saw what you just did and went and hammered on the door. Finally Tammy's awful useless dad came out, grunted something unintelligible at me, and went back inside. Tammy had a black eye the next day.'

'Jesus Christ,' I said.

The tiny girl had gone inside now, and the door was slowly closing behind her.

'That kid is three years old,' I said, more to myself than anyone else.

'Goin' on sixteen,' Arnold said. 'Homeward bound, ladies and gents. Hold on to your toupees.'

Five o'clock: the crèche was empty and the shadows growing long in the echoing room. I was bone tired, but knew there was one thing I still had to do before going home for the night. I sat at the work table in the play room, its surface still tacky from being wiped clean, and opened the slim file Little Scamps kept on Tammy.

Most early-years settings do not have much paperwork on the children, but I knew this one would be different – all the children were referrals from Child Services, and would have arrived with a fair amount of information accompanying them. As a rule I try to keep away from files because they contain opinions and conclusions drawn by other people, many of whom have had only the most cursory contact with the subject.

One of the distasteful truths about childcare work is that relationships are not equal in any meaningful way: the adults are always in a position of power, in terms of size and authority as well as in knowledge of the lives of the children with whom they work. A child in a crèche will know a little about the various staff members – some will be more open than others about their private lives – but almost every child-care worker will know a huge amount about the family and friends of all the children in their care. Children talk, and their innocence prevents them censoring their commentary. It all comes out – Mammy drank too much wine last night and had a headache this morning so Daddy had to bring me into crèche; my brother has smelly feet; my uncle is in prison . . . Nothing is sacred. Workers are governed by rules of confidentiality, but the imbalance remains. I was aware of it, but helpless to do much to redress it. If I wanted to make any real headway with Tammy, I was going to have to learn a bit more about her.

The file ran to about twenty pages, a quarter of which dealt with Tammy's birth and early infancy. There was a section on intervention by a social worker that had come to nothing, and a letter from a woman who ran a playschool near Tammy's home – it was she who was ultimately responsible for Tammy being in Little Scamps: she had written to Child Services when Tammy's conduct became unmanageable. I leafed through various pages, making notes as I went. I saw words like *aggressive* and *antisocial*. I read that Tammy was *intellectually subnormal* and exhibited *no social skills*. Yet nowhere did I see any assessments having been carried out to back up these assumptions, and absolutely no evidence of anything having been done to tackle such serious issues. In fact, it seemed to me that a lot had been done to help Tammy's parents while she had been allowed to stew in her own juice.

After an hour I was left with three names: Imelda Gibb, a public-health nurse who had worked closely with the family when Tammy was very little; Fiona Thomson, a social worker who had stepped in when Imelda moved on; and

Sonya Kitchell, who had managed the pre-school Tammy had attended before Little Scamps.

Other than these names, my trawl through the file had taught me nothing I did not already know. I hoped the three women might be able to fill in at least some of the vast gaps in my knowledge of this enigmatic child. I stood up, stretched, and put the file back in its cabinet in the office. I thought I might take Millie for a walk after dinner – I needed air and space.

9

It was six thirty by the time I got home. I was renting a little cottage, a one-bedroom affair with a bit of garden. The owner, a semi-retired farmer who lived on a neighbouring hill, had helped me to put up an enclosure for Millie, a development my new canine friend viewed with distaste.

As I pulled up in the Austin I could see her standing upright, staring directly at me, and as I got out of the car she began whining and growling at me in tones of complaint.

I let her out and she tore around the garden three times, finally stopping on the front lawn to mark her territory. I noted with resignation that my previously verdant grass was becoming pock-marked with burned patches where similar displays had occurred, and went inside to make supper.

In all the fluster of starting in Little Scamps I had neglected to do any grocery shopping, but a quick perusal of the freezer unearthed some diced beef, and the vegetable tray had a couple of dried-up onions and two shrivelled chillies. I stuck the beef into the microwave to defrost and then, with Millie following me in case I happened to drop anything edible, I went out to the garden to see if there was anything to offer to the pot.

My efforts were rewarded with two bay leaves, some

thyme and sage, a handful of spinach, a couple of oversized radishes and a smallish beet. Back inside I put a Niall Toner CD on the kitchen stereo and began to chop the herbs. Then I diced the vegetables. Millie kept a very close eye on all this activity, standing at my side, acutely aware that the slightest slip of my hand might send something tasty her way.

Ten minutes later the cottage was filling with the scent of dinner cooking, and Millie and I were sitting out back, me with a bottle of beer, she with her favourite cuddly toy, a rather evil-looking stuffed rabbit. I'd like to say she treated it with affection, but all of Millie's toys ended up shredded – the similarities between my dog and the children at Little Scamps were becoming disturbing.

The secret to a good chilli is to cook it long enough for the beef to get really tender, but not so long that it all turns to mush. I have found that, if you cut the beef up quite small, an hour just about does it. If you put some bread in to bake about fifteen minutes after the chilli starts to simmer and keep a watchful eye on the clock, everything should be ready at about the same time. So I sipped my beer, listened to Niall singing about walking on water, and closed my eyes.

I probably would have dozed – Millie's breathing told me she was already asleep – if a voice hadn't said, 'I hope that's our dinner I smell and not the dog's.'

Lonnie was perched on my garden wall. 'Can't you just come in the gate like a normal person?' I asked, pleased to see him.

'I'd be hugely insulted if anyone ever accused me of being a normal person,' my friend retorted, jumping down to the grass and marching across it.

Lonnie is just under four feet tall. He has a strong, handsome face with a pronounced brow and a shock of black hair that he wears quite long. He also has a pronounced hump on his right shoulder and dresses flamboyantly. When I first met him he favoured enormous hats, flowing trench-coats that would trail along the ground behind him and loud flared trousers. I have always assumed that this was primarily because he had spent most of his life locked away from prying eyes, 'protected' from mockery by a mother and maiden aunt who were embarrassed by his condition. Lonnie had passed the time reading fantasy novels, stories in which dwarfs were heroic and accepted, and his attire reflected this.

Since becoming a member of staff at Drumlin (and seeing how other people dressed) Lonnie had tempered his fashion sense slightly, but still leaned towards bright colours and an almost punkish desire to clash whenever possible. Today he was wearing a loose shirt that was bright orange down one side and electric blue down the other. This was matched with pink and white checked trousers and canary yellow Doc Marten boots. If the fashion police ever came upon him, he'd soon be serving a very lengthy institutional sentence.

'I've got a pot of chilli on,' I said. 'You want a beer?'

'What've you got?'

'Umm . . . Bavaria. It's Dutch, I think.'

Out of a bag he had slung across his shoulder he produced an amber bottle, some kind of Scotch – Lonnie favoured sin-gle malts. 'I'm sure you'll take a drop of this afterwards.'

'I might force some down.' I grinned. 'Get a beer and a chair. Dinner'll be half an hour or so yet.'

When he was settled beside me he leaned down and scratched Millie behind the ears. 'She seems to be settling in nicely. Has she house-trained you yet?'

'I'm a slow learner. How are things at Drumlin?'

'We're just about managing without you. We say a prayer every morning for your safe return and for the welfare of the poor children left to your tender mercies.' He took a slug of beer and nodded in satisfaction. 'How are you managing in your new position?'

'All right, so far,' I said. 'But I have a feeling that the children are sort of sizing me up. I don't think the axe has really fallen yet.'

'Do tell,' Lonnie said, leaning back in his chair, so the front two legs were in the air. He had remarkable balance.

I told him about my first couple of days at Little Scamps, about the staff's exhaustion and the general chaos.

'So your plan is to redecorate, and get the kids to help?' he said, peeling the label off his beer bottle.

'I can't change the kids in one go,' I said, 'but I can change the environment.'

'Mmm. And our little water baby is one of your charges?'

'Tammy, yeah.'

'How has she been with you?'

'You'd think she'd never ever set eyes on me before.'

'What's wrong with her, anyway?' Lonnie asked.

'No one seems to know,' I replied, and told him what I had seen at Tammy's house earlier that day.

'I'd guess neglect might have something to do with it, then,' my friend said.

'To begin with,' I agreed.

'So what are you going to do?'

'About Tammy?'

'About all of it,' Lonnie said.

'Finish decorating and then play it by ear.'

'What I like about that plan is its simplicity,' Lonnie said sagely.

'Kind of foolproof, isn't it?' I agreed. 'I also need to hire some extra staff, and that may be a problem.'

'Why?'

'Well, Susan and Tush have tried and failed to get any new

people to stay,' I explained, 'and I am, in fairness, supposed to be getting these children to settle down and feel safe and comfortable in the place. If I cause even more changes – particularly ones that don't last – I might end up making things worse.'

'Bit of a mess,' Lonnie said, deadpan. 'One might even go so far as to say that you've been a total disaster.'

'Thanks for the support.'

'You're welcome. Now, seeing as how I hauled my arse all the way over here on a very warm evening, is there any chance of you feeding me before I die of starvation?'

'Well, since you put it like that . . .' I said.

We went inside.

Dinner passed pleasantly, with no mention of work. Lonnie had seen very little of the world, but he was widely read and could talk on virtually any subject. This made him an enormously entertaining dinner companion. That evening I was treated to his theories about the latent homosexuality in Tolkien's *Lord of the Rings* (riddled with it, apparently), the real reason the French irritate so many people (how can a nation consider itself the pinnacle of art and culture when its greatest work of architecture is basically a bit of leftover scaffolding?), and whether or not Elvis was really dead (who cared?). When the plates were cleared away we took Millie for a short stroll through a pretty little wood near the cottage, where she spent her time chasing rabbits.

'What do you think she'd do if she ever caught one?' I asked Lonnie, as we watched the greyhound pounding helter-skelter after a bundle of grey with a white bobtail. As soon as it disappeared underground another (or maybe the same one) popped out of a hole ten yards to the left and Millie was off again.

'I expect she'd break its neck, disembowel it and eat the viscera,' Lonnie said, without a blink.

'Not the baby?' I said, aghast.

'Nature red in tooth and claw,' Lonnie said. 'It's instinct.'

By the time we got back to the cottage it was starting to get dark. I lit a small fire (it wasn't even slightly cold, but I always find a fire soothing and cheering), put some Miles Davis on the stereo and we sat nursing large whiskies.

'I've been thinking,' Lonnie said.

'I always find those words deeply disturbing,' I said.

'You should.'

'All right, I'll take the bait. What were you thinking about?'

'You need staff at this playschool, right?'

'We do.'

'How many do you need?'

'One will suffice. For now, anyway.'

'I'll do it.'

I took a swig of whisky. It was Teacher's – not a single malt but very mellow. 'That idea had never occurred to me,' I said, mulling the ins and outs of the proposal. 'You're qualified, aren't you?'

'I did a course last year. Tristan insisted on it.'

'And you have no criminal record.'

'Correct. And a piece of paper to prove it. As you well know, I haven't had much opportunity to get arrested in my uneventful life.'

I sat forward on my chair and looked at Lonnie seriously. 'Do you really want to leave Drumlin? I mean . . . it's all you've really known since . . . well, since . . .'

'Since you and Tristan found me,' Lonnie said tersely. 'Yes, I'm painfully aware of that. And it's one of the main reasons I want to throw my hat in with you. I want to strike out a little.'

'There are other ways,' I said. 'You could go to college, or take a holiday, or buy a cat. I appreciate what you're offering but—'

'Buy a cat?' Lonnie spluttered. 'Do you think I couldn't help?'

I heard the sharpness in his voice. I didn't want to hurt his feelings, but I owed it to him to be honest.

'I do. I think you'd be a huge benefit to me and the other staff, and the children would be lucky as hell to have you. But I need to know for certain that you aren't just jumping ship out of some misplaced sense of duty to me.'

'Why the fuck would I do that?' Lonnie said. 'I don't even like you.'

'I'm being serious,' I said, getting angry now myself. 'If you want me to go to Tristan and request that you be released, you have to be straight with me.'

'Okay.' Lonnie drained his glass and poured more. He held out the bottle to me, but I shook my head. 'If anything, *you* would be doing *me* the favour.'

'How so?'

Lonnie sat back and ran his hands through his hair. He was great at talking about anything other than his feelings – not unlike many of us, I suppose. 'When I came to Drumlin I was what you folks call a "trainee", a client, one of the people at the unit who needed help.'

'When I arrived there I needed help too,' I interjected. 'Not a damn thing wrong with that.'

'Yeah, but no one ever referred to you as disabled, or questioned your intellectual functioning, or tried to measure your social skills.'

I thought about a way to tell him he was wrong. But he wasn't. Finally: 'No. They didn't try to establish what was wrong with me.'

'Now don't get me wrong,' Lonnie said. 'The investigation wasn't done in a way that was intrusive or insulting. Anyway, I'm used to it. I've been the subject of comment and conjecture all my life. I've tolerated questions and probing about everything from my capacity to understand complex decimals to the size of my dick since I was a child. Tristan was, at least, sensitive about how he measured and classified me.'

'I'm not sure that's fair, Lonnie,' I said. 'No one tried to classify you.'

'Oh, so there was never any discussion at staff meetings as to what kind of dwarfism I have?'

'Well—'

'I know there was, Shane. Don't try and bullshit me!'

'I'm not—'

'You are! What classification of dwarfism do I have?'

'I don't fucking care what sort you have!'

'Tell me! Say it!'

We were shouting now. Millie had woken up and was pacing nervily. Lonnie patted the couch beside him and she jumped up, resting her head on his lap.

'You have achondroplasia,' I said, hating the sound of the word.

'What are the symptoms?' Lonnie asked, absently stroking Millie's head.

What killed me as I recited the scientific terminology was that, yet again, he was right. Tristan had a thick file detailing Lonnie's personal and medical history, including the specifics of his particular form of genetic abnormality. And I had made a point of visiting the medical section of the library of a local college where I taught an occasional class to see if I could learn anything extra. I told myself it was so I could help the angry little man, but it was nothing more than intellectual curiosity. And arrogance.

'What are the symptoms, Shane?' Lonnie repeated. 'I know you're well aware of them.'

'It's the most recognizable and the commonest form of dwarfism,' I said slowly, trying desperately to maintain eye contact. Looking away would just aggravate my embarrassment. 'It accounts for seventy per cent of dwarfism cases internationally. The physical manifestations are short limbs, but in some cases, like yours, abnormally long ones too.'

'Flattered you noticed,' Lonnie said, smiling.

'Also there can be increased spinal curvature – like in your . . . um . . . shoulder. And distortion of skull growth.'

'So how does one end up with achondroplasic dwarfism, then?' Lonnie asked. He was not going to let up.

'Achondroplasia is an autosomal dominant disorder caused by the presence of a faulty allele in a person's genome,' I said. 'If a pair of achondroplasia alleles are present, the result is fatal. One, though, causes the disorder in a live birth. Achondroplasia itself is a mutation in the fibroblast growth-factor receptor – gene three, I think, but don't quote me.'

'You're right,' Lonnie said. 'Explain how this mutated gene works.'

'Well, it's an inhibitor that regulates bone growth. In cases of achondroplasia, the gene is too aggressive, negatively impacting on bone growth. Tristan told me that it may be exclusively inherited from the father and becomes more common with paternal age, specifically males reproducing after thirty-five.'

'Funny, isn't it?' Lonnie said, as if he didn't find it funny at all. 'I never even knew the man who made me this way.'

I reached over for the bottle and poured myself a stiff drink, which I downed in two swallows. I needed to wash the taste of the conversation from my mouth.

'Why are you doing this, Lonnie?' I asked. 'How have I made you angry?'

'I'm not angry with you, you big lug,' he said. 'What hurts is that every single one of you – my friends and colleagues – have dissected me in just the way you did there. I am, to them, a medical display. Something to be analysed and tested.'

This was not going anywhere good.

'The reason I'm so set on getting a job somewhere other than Drumlin is that I want an opportunity to work somewhere where all that baggage doesn't exist, where I might actually be seen as a real person and not as an oddity – at least, no more so than I truly have to be.'

'You're not an oddity, Lonnie,' I said.

'Of course I am. My real complaint is that I'm so often seen as an oddity without a brain.'

'It would be great to say that was never the case,' I said slowly, trying to pick my words as carefully as possible, 'but, in truth, it probably was at one time. But it's not now. People see *you* – not your disorder, if you even want to call dwarfism a disorder. And let's be honest, Lonnie, you don't think of yourself like that.'

'Don't I?'

'No, you bloody don't!' I said. 'I know you pretty well, and all I've ever seen was you being proud of who you are. You don't hide away – you even dress to attract attention, for fuck sake.'

Lonnie tutted sadly. 'And has it never occurred to you that this may be a defence mechanism? If people are talking about my crazy clothes, perhaps they're not looking at my short, bowed legs or my simian, dangling arms or my hunched back?'

I didn't know how to respond to that. Of course it had occurred to me, but I had pushed the notion aside. I was fond of Lonnie, and the idea that he often felt lost, frightened and alone was more than I wanted to deal with. I preferred to believe that he was fixed – set on the road for a happy, healthy, fulfilled life. 'What do you want me to say?' I asked. 'I consider you one of my best friends. When I look at you I don't see a dwarf – I see a pig-headed, stubborn arsehole with lousy fashion ideas and a sense of humour that would make Roy Chubby Brown blush.'

He grinned.

'And I see someone with a whole lot of courage and a true, open heart,' I finished.

'Giss a job, then, you fucking hippie,' Lonnie said.

'On two conditions,' I said.

'What?'

'Tristan has to agree to release you,' I said.

'And the second?'

'You have to call me "boss".'

I dodged the shoe he flung in my direction, but he hit me with the CD case.

10

Imelda Gibb, the public-health nurse who had worked with Tammy and her family, was a matronly grey-haired woman in her late fifties. I met her in the canteen of the hospital she worked out of early on Monday morning. I sipped some of the disgusting coffee and chipped at a fruit scone that might have caused blunt-force trauma in the wrong hands. Imelda had a bowl of porridge. I admire porridge eaters. I know it's ridiculously good for you, but can't seem to develop a taste for it.

'How can I help you, Mr Dunphy?' my companion asked. 'I haven't worked with Tammy recently. I deal with many children, as you, no doubt, are aware.'

I had her contributions to the file with me, and riffled through them. 'Tammy is in a crèche for children with special needs,' I said. 'She's presenting with some unique behaviours.'

'Such as?'

I listed them.

Imelda Gibb listened intently. 'Is she autistic, do you think?'

'It's the obvious conclusion,' I agreed. 'But no. I don't think she is.'

'I have no other suggestions.'

I pushed Imelda's report across the table to her. 'You wrote this after your second visit to Kylie and Dale's home,' I said. 'What you saw there was enough for you to request regular contact over the next two months.'

'Yes.'

'Imelda, the work I do isn't always easy to explain,' I said. 'Often it's just poking about, learning whatever you can, until you come across something you think might be useful. I have a picture of what Tammy is like now, but you know how she was as a baby.'

'Why not ask her parents?'

I laughed drily. 'They aren't really very communicative, just now.'

Imelda grunted. 'I suppose I could have guessed that. What do you want to know?'

I was in. 'When did you first meet her?'

Imelda pushed her empty porridge bowl aside, and went and got the coffee pot. She replenished both of our cups ('It's dreadful stuff, but it's hot and it's got caffeine in it'), then sat down. 'Kylie was known to Social Services before she had Tammy,' she began. 'There are literally entire cabinets full of reports and references to her family in the social-work department. As you are no doubt aware, when a person from that background has a baby, it sets off automatic alarm bells, and certain mechanisms click into motion. I am part of those mechanisms.'

'Do you mind my asking what the . . . um . . . issues were that brought Kylie's family to the attention of Social Services?'

'The usual sort.'

'I wasn't aware there was a usual sort,' I said.

'Mostly neglect. There was an allegation of sexual abuse made against Kylie's father, but it allegedly occurred outside the family and was never proven.'

'And do you know anything about Dale's family?'

'As I recall, he had a police record – petty crime – but his family were not considered bad. He struck me as a young man who could have been quite intelligent if life had dealt him a better hand.'

'Okay,' I said. 'So you went to see Kylie and Tammy in the maternity hospital.'

'I did. Dale was there too, when I visited. The child was fine. She was a little small, only a shade over five pounds, but not dangerously underweight. She slept most of the time while I was there, and cried very little when she did wake up. Kylie struck me as a little overwhelmed by it all, but Dale made up for that. He was extremely interested in everything I had to say. He asked lots of questions, made me show him how to hold the child properly, discussed the various benefits of different brands of nappy. I got the impression he had bought and closely read several mother-and-baby books.'

'They don't do many father-and-baby ones,' I said.

'Mmm,' she said. 'It's a turn of phrase, really, isn't it?'

'An unfortunate one, some might say,' I said.

She waved it off. 'When I visited their home, I was struck by the fact that, though it was very well prepared for a baby, it was, to all intents and purposes, just a shell.'

'I don't follow,' I said.

'They had hardly any furniture, there didn't seem to be any food in the house that wasn't for the baby, and Kylie – well, I have to say that she wasn't coping. At all.'

'How so?'

'Dale was doing everything. Now, look, I'm not one of those women who feel that breast-feeding has to be forced on every single mother in some sort of awful guilt-trip. But subtle questioning showed that she had never even tried to make

57

it work. Dale was bottle-feeding the child using formula. He had proper sterilizing equipment – I had no issue with that. I felt very strongly that Kylie had opted out of any role with the baby.'

'But Dale was doing a good job?'

'Oh, he seemed to dote on Tammy.'

I scratched my head and looked through the papers I had brought. 'And how was Tammy?'

'Developmentally, I would say she was, if anything, a little advanced.'

'Physically? Intellectually?'

'She was only three months old, Mr Dunphy. Within the parameters I had to work with I would say she was a little ahead, but not abnormally so.'

'She seemed happy? Healthy?'

'Yes. I would have said so.'

'So why did you recommend extended contact with the family?'

'For Kylie,' Imelda said. 'I thought she needed support. I was of the opinion that she was profoundly postnatally depressed, and that Dale, while most certainly caring for the baby, was not really offering her a shoulder to lean on.'

'Did you talk to him about it?'

'He's a man, Mr Dunphy,' Imelda said, 'and therefore unlikely to experience something like post-natal depression.'

'Does masculinity mean a complete lack of empathy?' I asked.

'Sometimes,' Imelda said, 'I think it does.'

Despite any lingering reservations I might have had, Lonnie started at Little Scamps two days later, and our family was complete. Susan and Tush scarcely batted an eyelid when he walked in – they had seen too much strangeness in the children to be fazed by a garishly dressed dwarf. Tush, to my surprise and, if I'm honest, pride, pointed out that we now had gender balance within the staff team, which was something I had never even considered.

The day Lonnie was to start I went into work early and baked some scones. I had scheduled the first of our staff meetings and wanted to make sure everyone was as comfortable and happy as possible. If we were to function as a unit we needed to be very relaxed and open with each other, and that meant meetings had to be seen as occasions of absolute equanimity and free expression. Ben Tyrrell, an old boss, had taught me never to underestimate the value of a few cakes at such affairs.

When my three associates arrived I had the table in the kitchen laid out, and the whole place smelling warmly of baking.

When everyone was sitting comfortably, I kicked off the discussion. 'Okay,' I said. 'We've got a team in place and we're ready to start putting up murals. The kids have been as good as gold the last two days, with a few slight hiccups.'

'Sounds to me like we're winning,' Susan chimed in. 'At long last.'

'You'd think so, wouldn't you?' I asked. 'I mean, we have every reason to believe we've had a major breakthrough.'

'So why do you sound like you don't believe it?' Tush asked warily.

'He thinks they're biding their time,' Lonnie said. 'Waiting to see how we respond to things, gauging our weak spots.'

The eyes of the two women turned to Lonnie, who was spreading jam on a piece of scone. He didn't look up.

'That's kind of cynical,' Susan said. 'Aren't we meant to accentuate the positive and so on?'

'I'm all for that when it makes sense to do so,' I said. 'And right now I believe we'd be better off battening down the hatches and preparing for an onslaught.'

'I don't like the sound of that,' Tush said.

'Me neither,' I said.

Lonnie grinned at everyone. 'So when do the little darlings arrive?'

They arrived all too quickly, and we started the day with large circle time. Susan had flung the windows open and the sound of birds singing in the trees drifted in. With the walls fresh and white, the broken toys cleared out, the room seemed bright, airy and full of possibility. The kids sat in a ring, the staff dotted at various points among them.

'Good morning, everyone,' I said. 'I want to welcome you all here today, and to tell you that it is a special day. Can any of you tell me why?'

'It's my birthday,' Ross said, raising a crutch into the air as if it were an extension of his arm.

'It's not your birthday, Ross,' Susan said. 'You were born in November.'

'Happy birthday to me!' Ross sang, swinging his legs in time to the melody.

'Is it Christmas?' Mitzi asked, smiling sweetly.

'I think we might have mentioned to you that Christmas was coming,' I said patiently. 'I dare say you've noticed the ads on the TV, too.'

'*Holidays are coming, holidays are coming,*' Gilbert sang very quietly, but soon all the children (and Lonnie) had joined in merrily.

'No – you still haven't got it,' I said, when the group had settled again.

'Little fella?' Jeffrey pointed at Lonnie.

'His name is Lonnie,' I said. 'And, yes, he is part of the reason today is special.'

'That little man is a midget,' Milandra said vehemently. 'Like in *Willie Wonka*.'

'A little Oompa Loompa.' Mitzi sighed. 'Daddy, can I have an Oompa Loompa all for my very own?'

'D'you want to hear me sing the Oompa Loompa song?' Lonnie said, as if he thought this was the most sensible suggestion anyone could possibly make.

I looked at him, agog. I had never encountered him being quite so tolerant before and, as with the children, I had a sneaking suspicion he was lulling me into a false sense of security.

'Yeah! Sing it!' Rufus said. 'Just like in that film!'

'You want to hear it?' Lonnie said.

'Yeah!'

'You all sure?'

'Yeah!' from all sides.

'Well . . .' Lonnie stood up in his chair as if it were a stage. He spread his arms out, his legs together and his back straight, just like the Oompa Loompas in the classic 1970s film.

The children cheered and whooped. Lonnie cleared his throat. 'Here I go . . .'

All eyes were on him. Then: 'No.' Lonnie shook his head and looked unhappy. 'Sorry. I won't do it. Because it hurts my feelings.'

The kids stopped their cat-calling and whooping and went silent.

'You – what's your name?' He pointed at Rufus.

'None a your business,' Rufus snapped, looking just as hurt and angry as Lonnie.

'His name is Rufus,' I said.

'Rufus, do you know your colours?'

'Yeah.'

'Well, do I have orange skin?' Lonnie asked. There was no anger in his voice: he was teaching the children a lesson, and I was interested to see how well they took it, and how much they understood of what he would say to them.

Rufus squinted at my friend, then shook his head. No, Lonnie certainly did not have orange skin.

'What's your name?' He nodded at Mitzi.

'I am Mitzi. Mitzi, that's me.' The child smirked.

'Do I have blue hair, Mitzi?'

'Oh, no. You have lovely hair, little man. So soft and silky.'

'You,' at Gus.

'What?' Gus shot back.

'Do I work in a chocolate factory?'

'I don't know! Do you?'

'I work right here, at Little Scamps. With you.'

'So?' Gus spat.

'So I am obviously not an Oompa Loompa, am I? I also want to make sure you all know that I am not a Munchkin, one of Snow White's dwarfs – my name is not Sleepy or Dopey and even though I can be grumpy, you can't call me that – and I do not hang out with Orlando Bloom. Shane has long hair. Susan has green eyes. Tush is left handed. Everybody is different – I just happen to be smaller than most people.'

He looked at Milandra. 'Do you know that there are names for people with skin like yours that are very bad to say?'

'You mean "nigger",' she said. 'I know those names.'

'Well, calling me a midget is like calling you that. You shouldn't say it.'

She looked at him with huge eyes. I wondered if anyone had ever spoken to her like that before. 'Okay, little man.'

'Not that, either,' he said. 'I would never call you "black girl".'

'I *am* a black girl,' she said.

Lonnie grinned. 'And a very pretty one.'

I decided to intercede. 'I think what Lonnie is saying is very worthwhile for us all to listen to. It would be a good thing if we tried to be a little nicer to one another. But come on – you still haven't thought of the reason why today is such a special day. Will I tell you?'

Nods and yeses.

'Well, today is the first day we're all together in this group, and it's also the day we start painting our murals. So it's the beginning of two very exciting things.'

Arga jabbered something in Polish, but from her elaborate mime I guessed she wanted to talk about the painting.

I had come prepared. 'Okay,' I said, reaching under my chair. 'As you know, I want everyone to paint their own pictures, so you all have your special places on the walls around the room. But I have two ideas I'd like the whole group to get involved in. Here's the first one.'

From under my chair I pulled out a very large hardback book. I opened it at a centre page and held it up for all to see. 'This little guy,' I said, pointing to a beautiful painting of a rabbit in a bright blue jacket, 'is Peter. He lives in a part of England not unlike here – it's out in the country and there are lots of lakes and hills and woods. He has a mammy and a daddy, just like you, and sometimes he's a bit of a naughty rabbit, and gets into trouble.'

'I knows that rabbit,' Rufus said solemnly.

'Do you?' I asked. 'Maybe he and his family are in Ireland now.'

'They might be,' Ross said. 'I do see a lot of rabbits in the woods near my house.'

'He is a rabbit who enjoys a nice little coat,' Mitzi said.

'Mmm,' I agreed. 'I don't think I've ever seen a rabbit wearing clothes.'

'Me no see,' Jeffrey said.

'You've never seen that either?' I asked.

Jeffrey shook his head and worked his tongue. People often think that people with Down's syndrome have over-sized tongues, but that is not the case – their mouth cavities are smaller than normal, which gives the impression that the tongue is too large.

'Are you saying that maybe the rabbits wear clothes when we can't see them?' I asked Jeffrey.

He nodded, beaming.

'Well, that's possible,' I said. 'What do the rest of you think?'

This conversation continued to and fro. The idea of a colony of intelligent rabbits living nearby was just too delicious for any of them to pass up. I was just about to introduce the group to Beatrix Potter and her world of animals when I noticed that Tammy had gone – her chair was empty. I waited until Tush was discussing the myth about rabbits favouring carrots (they generally prefer lettuces and brassicas and will leave carrot crops largely untouched), then handed the book to her and made my way into the kitchen. Sure enough, through the still partly open door I could see the child sitting on the table munching a scone. She had her back to me, and was so involved in cramming the food into her mouth that she didn't hear me enter the room.

'You know, those are much better hot, with butter and jam,' I said, pulling out a chair and sitting down near her. I didn't want to get too close – her eyes were those of a cornered animal. 'Would you like me to pop one into the microwave and put some on it for you?'

She just eyed me and did not respond, which I decided to interpret as 'Yes please, Shane,' so I took one, put it on a plate and stuck it in to heat.

'I bet you'd also like some milk to drink,' I said. I poured some into a plastic cup and put it on the table next to her. She swiped it up and gulped half of it down without pausing. As she drank the rest I took the scone from the oven and spread it with butter and jam. When I had cut it up into bite-sized chunks I sat down and watched her eat. I didn't have to watch for long – the entire plate was empty within thirty seconds. 'You're pretty hungry, Tam,' I said.

She nodded. I had to fight the urge to punch the air and whoop – she was, in her way, talking to me.

'Like some more?'

The nod again. Pleased beyond words that I had opened even this basic line of communication, I got up and prepared another scone for her.

'Did you have any breakfast this morning?' I asked, as she scarfed it down.

She looked at me with eyes that almost held offence. Then, tentatively, she shook her head.

'Do you ever get breakfast?' My heart went out to her – she was so small, such a tiny little soul, but so self-sufficient, so tough. She paused, considering the question. Her head lolled from one side to the other as she thought about how to answer. I helped her: 'Sometimes?'

She shrugged in an exaggerated manner.

'But hardly ever,' I said, and she nodded firmly. I almost laughed. Tammy, although she chose not to speak, was a gifted communicator. 'Would you like it if I sorted it out for you to have some breakfast when you got into Little Scamps every day?'

An expression of fear came over her face, and she shook her head.

'Suppose I fixed it so nobody knew things were tough at home.'

She stopped eating and thought for a moment, studying the piece of scone in her hand as if it held the secrets to the universe. Then she gave me an expression that was certainly not a smile – I was beginning to think she didn't know how to smile – but involved a slight turning up of the corners of her mouth, a twitching of her eyes. Later I learned that this was her expression for pleasure and satisfaction.

'So we have a deal,' I said, reaching out and patting her shoulder. She froze momentarily when I touched her, and I made a mental note to keep such displays of affection to a minimum. She got over the paroxysm quickly though, and I felt a rush of fondness for the sad, silent child. It was an affection I would have to remind myself of often in the coming months.

11

As I had begun to explain to the group, the first project I had planned was based around Beatrix Potter's Peter Rabbit stories. I had been a huge fan of her tales as a child. I realize now that this seemingly quaint Victorian lady, with her amazingly detailed paintings and succinct text, was actually ploughing a deceptively dark and complex furrow through the consciousness of her youthful readers.

While her stories deal with funny animals that generally walk on their hind legs, wear clothes and engage in very human activities, there is still a sense that they live in a world where death and injury are just around the corner. The children at Little Scamps reminded me of Potter characters. They seemed small, cute and helpless, yet there was a well of resourcefulness and guile in each of them, and although they were very much at the mercy of the adults about them, each had a finely tuned survival instinct.

After a break for play outdoors, I read *The Tale of Peter Rabbit* aloud to the kids. I'd had full colour enlargements of the pictures made so they could all see them, and Susan held them up one by one. The story is simple: Peter Rabbit, his sisters, Flopsy, Mopsy and Cottontail, and his mother live in a rabbit hole under a fir-tree. Mother Rabbit has forbidden her children to enter the garden of Mr McGregor, a local small-holder, because their father had met his untimely end there and become the main ingredient of a pie. However, while Mrs Rabbit is shopping and the girls are collecting blackberries, Peter, rebellious soul that he is, sneaks into the garden. There, he gorges on vegetables until he gets sick, and is chased by Mr McGregor. When Peter loses his jacket and shoes, Mr McGregor uses them to dress a scarecrow. Eventually Peter escapes and returns to his mother, exhausted and feeling ill. She puts him to bed with a dose of camomile tea while his sisters (who have been good little bunnies) enjoy bread and milk and blackberries for supper.

The children listened, transfixed. I love telling stories, and find myself getting lost in them just as much as the children. Storytelling should be a performance, and I make a point of giving each character a different voice and the occasional gesture – children have a remarkable memory for such fea-tures, pointing out to me on repeat tellings if I get a voice wrong.

I chose *Peter Rabbit* as our first 'big' story because I know that children can identify with him. He is inherently a good soul, just a bit excitable and naughty, but not in a malicious way. He steals the contents of Mr McGregor's garden, but he *is* a rabbit, and is only doing what he is programmed to do.

Despite walking upright and wearing his blue jacket, the images of him in the book are all anatomically correct – he is clearly a wild rabbit, just like the ones my audience saw almost every day, and that eased things, too. This was not a story about trolls or goblins or even lions and tigers: it dealt with things that the kids had only to look outside their kitchen windows to see.

When I was finished, I put the book down, but Susan and I laid the pictures out in sequence on the floor, so the children could follow them as a kind of photo-essay while we talked.

'Do you think Peter is a good rabbit?' I asked.

'No, not good,' Jeffrey said flatly. 'Bold boy.'

'Why do you think he's bad?' I asked.

'Mammy say,' Jeffrey was puffing and panting with the effort of expressing what he wanted to articulate, 'no steal.'

'If I was a rabbit,' Lonnie said, 'and I passed a garden full of lovely fresh veg, I think I'd find it very hard not to go in and take some.'

'Berries,' Jeffrey said.

'That's right,' I agreed. 'His sisters went out and picked blackberries, didn't they? So there was food that could be taken without having to steal.'

'And his mammy worried about him goin' in that garden,' Gus said.

'Why did she worry, Gus?' Tush asked.

'Because Peter's dad had an accident in there,' Gus said.

'What kind of accident, do you think?' Susan asked.

The group sat quietly, thinking about that.

'Well, in the story, it says his daddy ended up in a great big pie,' Mitzi said. 'How could that have happened?'

'Mr M'Gregor,' Ross said. 'He kilt 'im, I'd say.'

'Why would he want to do that?' I asked.

'Peter robbin' the veg'ables,' Rufus said.

'So do you think Mr McGregor is right to try and kill Peter, and to kill and eat his father?' I asked.

I was met with a resounding silence. This was far too complex a moral dilemma for the group. The problem was clear: it was naughty of Peter to steal the vegetables because stealing is wrong and therefore should be punished. Yet Peter was a nice rabbit, and the children felt a strong sense of solidarity with him. How then was it all right for anyone to kill either Peter or members of his family, even to eat them for dinner?

Arga was looking at the picture of a Peter who, having lost his clothes and believing himself to be trapped in the garden, is crying bitterly. The image seemed to have stirred something in the child, who had begun to speak loudly in Polish. She was pointing at the picture, and Gilbert, who was, as usual, beside her, placed a hand on her arm.

'Arga, honey, I don't know what you're trying to say,' I said.

'*Arrrrgaaaa!*' she said angrily, rolling those *r*s for me (our constant mispronunciation of her name irritated her greatly), then continued to talk rapidly.

Lonnie hopped off his chair and went over to her. In quiet tones he spoke to her: '*Co się stało, kochanie?*' I later learned this was Polish for 'What's wrong, sweetheart?'

At what sounded like a hundred miles per hour Arga rattled something back.

'*Powoli,*' Lonnie said, patting the air rhythmically with his hand: slowly.

'*Został pozostawiony sam sobie,*' Arga said, tears streaming down her face now.

I waited with bated breath – this was wholly unexpected. It was as if Lonnie had just produced a rabbit from a hat.

'She says that he has been left all alone,' Lonnie translated.

'Do you speak Polish?' I asked disbelievingly.

He turned to look at me with a halfway grin on his face. 'And the prize for asking the most obvious question imaginable goes to the long-haired gentleman. Yes, I speak a bit of Polish.'

'Umm . . . when were you going to tell me that fascinating little nugget of information?'

'When were you going to tell me you had a child here who speaks Polish fluently but has not one word of English?'

I stopped for a moment. 'I thought I had.'

Lonnie shook his head impatiently, then turned back to Arga. '*Znasz jego mammy znajduje go.*' You know Peter's mammy finds him.

'*Może nie na długo,*' Arga said. '*I on będzie smutny i przestraszony.*'

'But maybe too late,' Lonnie relayed to us. 'And he will be cold and frightened.'

Lonnie spoke to her, turning her to face him. I saw a kind of relief spread across Arga's face: someone finally understood her and was taking the time to reassure and comfort her.

'*Nie chciałbym do tego dopuścić do ciebie, kochanie. Jesteś bezpieczny, teraz.*' I wouldn't let that happen to you, sweetheart. You're safe, now.

The child threw her arms around Lonnie's neck and hugged him tightly, sobbing loudly. He hugged her back, then picked her up in his powerful arms and went back to his chair, Gilbert following them like a lapdog. As he settled back into his place, I saw that tears were running down his cheeks, too. Lonnie sat for the rest of the session with Arga on one knee, and Gilbert perched on the other, the latter obviously uncomfortable with the physical contact, but determined not to leave his friend.

It was not until I got home that evening and pondered the events of the day – and it would prove to be a long and eventful one – that I realized just how much Arga and Lonnie had in common: she an abandoned, semi-feral child; he a modern-day and very real fairy-tale character, whose family had, in a slightly more benign way, abandoned him, too. He had been locked in the attic room when his mother died and his aunt, finding the body, had died of shock. It had been days before a workman had called and found Lonnie, terrified and half starved in his prison. I thought about them both, that night, as I lay in the darkness and felt the hours tick away: unloved children in a difficult, cruel world. And wondered if there was anything anyone could ever do other than extend friendship and hope for the best.

It is a question to which I do not think I have ever received an answer.

Another question without an answer was Tammy: she was by far the hardest of the children to read. Milandra was the firebrand; Gus the joker; Julie the vulnerable waif. Who, then, was Tammy?

It took hours of close observation to grasp that she did not really have a role, other than that of outsider. The other children (who barely had time for one another as it was) ignored her, and she generally behaved as if they weren't there either, unless she wanted something – a toy or book, usually – that someone else had. Then her violence could be truly shocking. Children can be cruel, and rough-and-tumble is a daily occurrence in any crèche, but Tammy's assaults on her peers could border on the psychotic.

She thought nothing of using weapons, and the other kids had become adept at getting out of her way when they saw her coming – *if* they saw her coming. Tammy never spoke and hardly ever cried out in anger or pain, but she also moved with little or no sound. I once watched her running from one end of the playroom to the other when the other children were out in the yard; I interpreted it as a rare physical expression of joy, but knew in my heart that she was just as likely to be burning off energy. During this outburst of activity she never made a single noise. Had I not been watching her closely, I wouldn't have known she had budged an inch.

The absence of sound was mirrored by a complete lack of emotional response. Tammy never seemed angry or frightened, happy or sad, amused or bored. She just ... *was*. I knew from observing her that she liked books and favoured the book corner above all other spaces in Little Scamps, simply because that was where she went when not directed to go anywhere else, but truth be told, she displayed as much contentment sitting at the table doing art, or standing in the corner of the yard outside or hanging about in the kitchen waiting for one of us to give her lunch.

Her reticence made forming a relationship with her extremely difficult. We base our own emotional responses on the feedback we receive from those about us. When we interact with another person, all our perceptions of how that communication is developing are rooted in what we feel our counterpart is projecting at us. When that reference point is removed, we have very little to go on, and this causes discomfort.

I'm not ashamed to admit that a large part of me initially balked at trying to bond with Tammy. If she didn't want to be friends with me, why should I make any effort with her? Almost as soon as these thoughts drifted through my mind, I recognized how childish and selfish they were. And I began to ask some important questions.

Why would anyone go to such lengths to isolate themselves from their fellows? The only answer that presented itself was that such a person must have been so cruelly and harshly rejected that they harboured a deep-rooted terror of experiencing such pain again, and went to extremes to be unapproachable. As a childcare worker, it was very much my duty to break through this crust of antagonism and forge some links.

It was unlikely to be an easy proposition.

12

'You want us to do *what*?' Susan asked. She uttered the last word in a whisper that seemed so closely to resemble a shout that I wondered if it could technically be classified as anything else.

It was lunchtime, and we were sitting at various points in the outdoor area. The kids were all eating their sandwiches – I had made some for Tammy, who had brought none with her.

'I want to go on a nature walk,' I said.

'Where?'

'There's some fields and woodland about half a mile north of here,' I said. 'I think it'd be great for the children to see some real rabbits in the wild.'

'And wouldn't it be great for us to lose four or five of them into the bargain?' Susan said. 'And it'd be even more great to get sued by their parents and lose our jobs.'

'Am I detecting sarcasm in that last statement?' Lonnie asked, without looking up from the book he had open on his knees.

'Whatever gives you that idea?' Susan snapped.

'Oh, there it goes again,' Lonnie muttered absently.

'And how are we going to get there?' Susan asked.

'I thought we might walk,' I said. 'You know, walk, nature walk – they sort of complement each other.'

'Now who's being sarcastic?' Susan asked.

'Don't you think it'll do them good?' I was annoyed at her reaction.

'Of course I do, but weren't you the one this morning saying we should expect an explosion? I'm a big believer in keeping such things contained, if at all possible.'

'I can see where you're coming from, but I also reckon we should start as we mean to continue,' I said. 'If we ever want to be able to take this crowd for trips into the outside world, we have to start somewhere. Why not now?'

Susan glowered at Lonnie, who still had his head stuck in the latest George R. R. Martin book, a tome that looked as if it weighed as much as he did. 'What do you think, newbie?' she asked him.

'I'm with him,' Lonnie said, still not looking at either of us.

'What do you mean?' Susan retorted.

'I mean,' Lonnie said, shaking his head in vexation, folding over the top corner of the page he was reading and closing the paperback, 'that I came here to work with the hippie there. If he wants to bring us on a nature walk, or a moon walk, or a cake walk, I'll go along.'

'What if he's wrong?' Susan said. She sounded despairing.

'Then we'll deal with that and make fun of him afterwards,' Lonnie said, smiling.

'Can't we just make fun of him now and be done with it?'

'That's not how it's done.' Lonnie chuckled.

'Things would be a lot easier if they were,' Susan said.

'But so much less fun,' Lonnie riposted.

13

The kids filed along the road two by two, each holding the hand of a partner.

The only fly in the ointment was Mitzi, who simply could not walk more than ten yards without a rest. For her we brought a wheelchair, but I insisted that she walk at least some of the way, which meant that Ross could use the chair if he needed to during the periods when she was not squeezed into it. The problem with Ross, of course, was that he didn't want to use the chair at all, even when sweat was trickling down his face in rivulets and he was nearing exhaustion. I admired his spirit – as far as he was concerned he didn't have a disability – but it wasn't practical to let him walk all the way: at times he needed to rest.

The result was that Mitzi plodded doggedly along the road in front of me, holding hands with Gus, who tolerated her grimly. She panted heavily, muttering threats in her sing-song, baby voice: 'Oh, yes, children, he might get pushed out under a car, if he's not careful.' Or: 'Spit in his lunch, I might. Yes – get some poop and put it in his sandwiches. We could do that.'

Knowing that she was not beyond such things, I decided to check my food carefully in future.

Lonnie was beside me as we walked – we'd decided not to hold hands – and he found Mitzi's smiling tirade of abuse hilarious.

'You're a secretive sonofabitch, aren't you?' I said, as we strolled along.

'How so?'

'Wouldn't you say that keeping the fact that you speak Polish like a true-born fucking Pole might come as something of a surprise to me?'

Lonnie sniffed. 'Oh. That.'

'Where'd you learn it?' I was fascinated.

I had been under the impression that throughout his childhood he had never left the old town house his mother and aunt had shared, and had then moved to his tiny cottage on the mountain and been a veritable hermit there. I could not see how the opportunity to learn a foreign language – much less one as unusual as Polish – had ever presented itself.

'Did I ever tell you about when my mother sent me to the home?' he said at last.

'An institution of some sort?'

'I suppose you academics might call it an industrial school.'

'No – I don't think Tristan's aware of it either.'

'I'm certain he is,' Lonnie said. 'Just 'cause he never told you doesn't mean he doesn't know.'

I couldn't argue with that, so I didn't. 'Do you want to tell me about it?' I asked.

'Not really,' Lonnie said, stopping to pluck a blade of meadow grass from the roadside hedge. He stuck the end into the corner of his mouth to chew. 'It was a pretty horrible time. Thanks be to God my mother visited regularly, and when she saw I was gradually becoming ill from starvation and various other forms of abuse, she took me home. It was a kindness I shall never forget.'

'She did send you there in the first place, mate.'

'Due to the advice of a lot of people she had been brought up to trust – the local GP, the parish priest, a psychiatrist . . . It was the done thing, back then.'

We walked on a bit. It was a glorious afternoon – when the weather is good, Ireland is the best place in the world to be.

'Were you with priests or nuns?' I asked, after a while.

'Nuns.'

'And they taught you to speak Polish?' I asked incredulously. He snorted.

'Not going to give up, are you?'

'No, sir.'

'It was in Dublin, a home for people with physical and intellectual disabilities. We were treated well enough, a lot of the time. I know I was lucky – some of the schools in Dublin used children for medical experiments and surgical trials but I was spared that. Food was withheld as a punishment, and we were beaten. There were some adults there – not all of them religious – who took pleasure in tormenting us, but the majority were not bad people.'

'You're far more charitable than I would be,' I said.

'Hate can eat you up if you let it,' Lonnie said philosophically.

'Yeah, I've heard that,' I said noncommittally.

'I'd been at the school for six months when Sister Angelica came. I don't know what age she was, but she looked to me to be in her early twenties. She was the most beautiful thing I'd ever seen.'

'And she was Polish,' I said.

'Yes. Poland has always been a strongly Roman Catholic country, even during the Communist occupation,' Lonnie said, as if he was giving a lecture.

'Really?'

'Yeah. You know Pope John Paul the Second was Polish?'
'Yes.'
'Sister Angelica came to us because she had been on a foreign mission in the Congo and had become ill. We were never told, but I've always believed she'd had malaria. She was transported to Ireland because we have a temperate climate. To convalesce.'
'And you had a crush on her.'
Lonnie grinned. 'Anyone would have. She wasn't a teacher, she was just sort of . . . about. She'd walk around the perimeter of the playing fields, saying her rosary or reading her missal. One day I plucked up the courage and asked if I could walk with her. She looked at me oddly for a second, then said, "Come, my *krasnoludek*." That was what she always called me.'
'What does it mean?' I asked, curious.
'There isn't really a clear English equivalent. The *krasnoludek* is a sort of Polish forest creature, different from a dwarf or a gnome, although some of the books I've read depict it in a very similar way. It's completely good, and will help people if it can. A sort of benign spirit of the wilderness, I suppose.'
'Rather a pagan thing for a good Catholic nun to say, don't you think?'
'Angelica was from the mountains – she grew up steeped in the old folk tales and stories. I sometimes wondered if she really did think I was a *krasnoludek*, sent to look after her.'
'How did she start to teach you her mother tongue?' I wondered.
'She didn't have great English, so she would often use Polish words out of necessity. I started to ask her to say them to me slowly and point at whatever it was she wanted, or mime it out, and I'd give her the English version – so we ended up sort of teaching one other. I picked up quite a bit in

the six months I was with her, and when I got home I asked my mother to get me some Polish grammar and vocabulary primers. Like I told you before, she never refused me a book.'

'When you left the school did you ever see Angelica again?' I asked.

He laughed bitterly. 'No. Despite everything that was going on, would you believe that I actually asked my mother to let me stay in the home?'

'So even though you argued and begged to stay, she made you leave?' I said. 'I would guess she took a stand because she knew you needed to get out of there.'

Lonnie nodded. 'I think about Angelica every day, though,' he said.

'The one who got away,' I said.

'That would suggest I caught her, even for a short while,' Lonnie said.

'True,' I said. 'But you did love her, and it sounds as if *she* needed a friend very much, and you were it. So I guess she loved you, too, in her way. Just because you didn't go all Lady Chatterley in the woodshed doesn't mean you didn't care about each other. And it would have been highly inappropriate if you had done, anyway. Take it for what it was – you had a special relationship with this woman, and it was broken off before it had run its course. That's a tragedy.'

'I wonder where she is now,' Lonnie said, and we spoke about it no more for a while.

14

I knew that the children would get a kick out of the rabbits for perhaps ten minutes, and that we had to plan something else to keep them amused for the other forty we would be in the woods. We had brought along a backpack with items for a treasure hunt, some bags for the kids to collect bits and pieces for a nature table I was hoping to establish in the playroom, and there was always hide-and-seek and chase if things got really bad.

The bunnies did not disappoint. Beatrix Potter would have loved the woods: a path that looked as if it had been created by rabbit workmen led to a small clearing, and as we made our way down this natural walkway I could already see a throng of rabbits playing, resting and eating in the open space ahead.

Of course they scattered as soon as we arrived, but Tush, who knew the area well, told us all to sit down quietly and have our juice (I had brought some cartons), and they might come back. To my utter surprise, the group sat in complete silence and waited, sipping through their straws. Within three minutes Gus hissed, '*Over there!*'

From behind a grey ash tree a little brown face was peering, its nose twitching.

'*And over there!*' Milandra shouted, which sent both animals scooting for cover.

'You need to be as quiet as you can,' Tush said. 'That means no shouting, okay?'

Moments later Arga said: '*Tam!*' There!

Soon we were surrounded, and not just by rabbits. Two grey squirrels, which seemed to be almost tame – or were much braver than Peter and his friends – ran about the children's feet, looking for food, and a robin perched on a stump nearby.

'Why does none of them have jackets?' Rufus asked.

'Well, I think rabbits only really wear jackets in storybooks,' I said.

'So is that book a lie?' Gus asked.

I had not expected this line of questioning. 'Well ... it's more like using your imagination,' I said. 'If you could understand what a rabbit said, what might that be like?'

'So the Potty lady maked it up?' Mitzi said.

'She did, but all the animals she drew were based on animals she had as pets or who came to her garden. So Peter was a real rabbit.'

'Was he her friend, then?' Rufus asked, his face contorted in serious concentration – he was trying hard to make sense of all this.

'Yes, he was,' I said. 'Beatrix Potter lived in the country, just like here, and she was fascinated by all the animals and plants she saw. She didn't just draw and write stories – she used to write books about nature too, and scientists and teachers read them and thought they were very good. So she was a very clever lady.'

'Why'd she write them kids' books if she was so brainy?' Milandra wanted to know. 'If'n I was a real brainy woman I wouldn' write no books for no dumb kids.'

'Why not?' I asked. 'I have books at home that I've had ever since I was younger than you, and I still read them. They're some of the most precious things I have. I'd much prefer to write books like that than some boring old science paper that people read because they have to.'

'And you can learn stuff from stories,' Ross said, his eyes locked on a big rabbit that was sitting, seemingly dozing, maybe five feet from him.

'That's very true,' I said. 'What did you learn from the *Peter Rabbit* story, Ross?'

'If you don't do what your mammy tells you, you can get in bad trouble,' Ross said. 'And not trouble like being gev out to, but trouble like where you can get hurt.'

'Peter nearly got caught by Mr McGregor, didn't he?' Susan said. 'And we all know what would have happened then.'

'Dead,' Ross said gravely.

'Maybe Peter went into the garden *because* of what happened to his da,' Gus said.

We all looked at him.

'What do you mean?' I asked him.

'Well, when my daddy goes out, my gran always says to me, "Gus, you de man of de house now." See, Peter is the only boy left in his house, isn't he?'

'He is.' I nodded.

'Maybe he was goin' in that garden to get food for his mam and his sisters. Like his dad done.'

'To be the provider,' I said.

'Yeah. De man of de house,' Gus said. 'But then he got scared, and he forgot to bring any food home.'

'Do you think it would be scary to be the man of the house, Gus?' Lonnie asked.

'Well – you wouldn't get to play much, I s'pose,' Gus said. 'You'd have to work and make money an' stuff.'

'Would that be fun?' Tush asked.

'It might be,' Ross said. 'If you was a soccer player or in a band.'

'Yeah!' Jeffrey said. 'Me guitar!' And he stood up and played a mean air guitar, providing some sound effects that sent every creature in the clearing scattering. None of us minded, though – in that short time the children had touched on some interesting and quite difficult ideas. I watched Jeffrey and Gus rock out, and it was then that I noticed Tammy had disappeared again.

15

It's funny how rapidly things can fall asunder, and how completely an afternoon that has been, up to a certain point, going swimmingly can transform into a nightmare.

As soon as I noticed Tammy had slipped away I proposed a treasure hunt. I didn't think she had gone far, and thought that the promise of finding some sweets might flush her out of wherever she was. While Lonnie hid the little bags of sugar-free jellies at various fairly easily spotted locations about the clearing we all sang a few verses of 'She'll Be Coming Round The Mountain'. Lonnie gave me the nod that the payload had been delivered, and I announced loudly that the hunt was on. The kids scuttled off, squealing with delight.

'Tammy's gone,' I said to Susan, discreetly, as soon as the kids were busy.

'I know,' she said. 'Don't say I didn't warn you.'

'I'm going to have a scoot around and see if I can find her,' I said. 'I won't be long.'

She nodded, and I jogged off into the trees.

I kept within a radius of around a hundred yards of the clearing. I called to her quietly, checked under hedges, even looked down what must have been the entrance to a badger's sett. I was gone for fifteen minutes, and could hear from the noise that carried in the still forest air that the group had finished the treasure hunt and had moved on to hide-and-seek.

Cursing my own stupidity I began to move back towards the group. Then the screaming started. I broke into a run.

When I got back to base camp, Lonnie and Tush were lying on the ground, trying to reach beneath a large bush that seemed to be part bramble, part laurel. Susan was organizing the rest of the kids into lines for a relay race.

'What's going on?' I asked.

'Mitzi,' Tush said.

'What has she done?' I sighed.

'Sweets were just about the worst thing we could have used for the treasure hunt,' Tush said. 'During the hunt she managed to snatch bags from Gilbert and Jeffrey. Then she took a run at Julie.'

I glanced about the group – Julie was absent, too.

'Arga tried to stop her,' Lonnie said, 'so, like some monster out of a horror movie, Mitzi grabbed Julie and dragged her into this bush.'

'What?' I asked in disbelief.

'Had to be seen to be believed,' Lonnie agreed. 'But she did it.'

I was losing my temper now – never wise in this line of work – but everything Susan had warned me about was happening, and I felt an idiot. I was worried about Tammy – and Mitzi, I decided, was a spoilt, over-indulged child who needed to be brought into line.

'Mitzi, that's quite enough nonsense. Leave Julie alone and come out right this minute,' I said sharply.

'Oh, he's such an arsehole, such an arsehole,' a high-pitched sing-song voice drifted out.

I could just hear Julie sobbing.

'Nice job,' Lonnie said. 'Maybe we should threaten to give her a whipping when she comes out.'

'Shut up, Lonnie,' I snapped.

'Yessir, boss, sir,' he said, effecting a salute.

Tush sniggered.

I lowered myself to the ground and peered under the bush. 'Can we get in there?' I asked Tush.

'No,' she said. 'If we had a machete or something we might be able to cut our way in, but she's managed to wedge herself into some kind of a hollow.'

'We could smoke them out,' Lonnie said. 'Shall I start gathering brushwood?'

'Shut up, Lonnie,' I reiterated.

Julie screamed again. I dreaded to think what Mitzi might be doing to her in there.

'Going to hurt the little retarded girl, oh, yes,' Mitzi sang. 'Shouldn't have made me walk like that.'

Julie screeched. The bush shook slightly, and then the sound stopped abruptly, as if it had been choked.

'Would you call this a Mexican standoff or, to borrow a term from the wacky world of chess, a stalemate?' Lonnie asked nonchalantly, and walked off into the trees.

I ignored him and began to try to squeeze into the space. If I pushed the scrub up with both hands I could just about make out a patch of darkness where the children must have crept. If I could get near it, I might get my arm in and haul them out. I figured that Mitzi might bite me or jab me with something sharp, but I could put up with that if we could get Julie out of her clutches.

The flaw in my plan was that a network of thick brambles and thorns had snaked its way across the entire distance I had to traverse, creating a kind of prickly spider's web. Within moments of attempting to shove my way through I was badly scratched and inextricably entangled. Driven by sheer panic, I decided to rely on brute force, and tried to haul the tendrils out by the root. Useless. Things were not looking good.

I had all but given up, and was just lying there in the dark, listening to Mitzi humming the theme music of *Hannah Montana* when someone grabbed me by the ankles and hauled me out in one swift movement.

'Stand aside and let the grown-ups work,' said Lonnie (for it was he).

He was holding a long, thick stick with a branch on the top turned in, like a hook. He bent down to the space he had just wrenched me out of and thrust the pole inside. He shoved it as far as he could, then took a deep breath and scooped it back out, bringing the brambles and vines with it, caught about the hook. He repeated the exercise three times, and cleared the space.

'Well, I'll be . . .' I said. Tush applauded.

Mitzi had become notably quiet during this exercise. Lonnie got down on his hands and knees, then lowered himself in a sort of half push-up. When he had satisfied himself that the passageway was safe, he scooted in.

'He's quite a guy, isn't he?' Tush said.

'He is that,' I agreed, though my voice belied the jealousy I felt – Lonnie was behaving confidently and assuredly while I looked like a bumbling fool.

The sounds of a scuffle emitted from the gap, and then Lonnie emerged, grubby, his hair flecked with leaves and bark. Julie was wrapped about his neck.

'Can I suggest we leave Mitzi in her fort for the moment?' he asked. 'I think she may come out of her own accord before too long.'

I watched as he trudged over to the rest of the group, Julie clinging to him for dear life.

'The little one will pay,' Mitzi sang in her hideout. 'They will all be sorry.'

'At least she's consistent,' I said to Tush.

We followed Lonnie. Tammy was still missing, and it was almost time to go back to Little Scamps.

16

The group reconvened a short distance away from Mitzi's hideout, minus Tammy and the by now solidly entrenched Mitzi.

I felt terrible. Everything that had happened was my fault. I had blundered into Little Scamps and experimented recklessly with the children's wellbeing, selfishly jeopardizing their safety and happiness.

I stood with my head bowed, at a loss as to what I should do and feeling very sorry for myself. I was aware that Susan and Tush were organizing the kids into their two-by-two line, and I could vaguely hear Lonnie talking quietly to Julie, who was still nestled into his shoulder. I was suddenly aware that, as things had progressed, my jealousy and anger towards Lonnie had grown. While my first few days at Little Scamps had closely resembled a bull's progress through a china shop, he seemed to exude authority and flair. Somewhere at the back of my mind I heard a voice muttering that I was supposed to be the qualified, experienced one. *I* was meant to be guiding *him*. I was ashamed of these thoughts immediately, but I couldn't unthink them.

'What are we going to do about Tammy?' Lonnie said.

I was so wrapped up in my misery that I did not respond.

'Shane, snap out of it, will you?'

'What?' I turned to look at him.

'Tammy's still out there somewhere.'

I rubbed the back of my neck, where I had been particularly badly mauled in my abortive attempt to get to Julie and Mitzi. The trees about us were silent. No animals frolicked hither and yon; the entire place was cold and uninviting.

'Let's head back to the road, and see if she follows,' I said, devoid of any other ideas.

'That was kind of my idea for Mitzi, too,' Lonnie said, winking. 'Come on, everyone,' he said loudly, directing his voice at the hole into which the child had disappeared. 'Let's go back to Little Scamps and have some tea and biccies before home-time. Did I see you had some chocolate ones, Tush?'

Tush blinked, uncertain what was going on, but then she caught up with Lonnie's train of thought. 'Oh, yes. There might be some at the back of the press in the kitchen.'

'Oh, good!' Lonnie said. 'They'll be nice, won't they, Shane?'

'Lovely,' I replied, without inflection.

This entire conversation was shouted, to ensure the words carried into the bowels of Mitzi's lair. Lonnie proceeded to stomp down the path, Susan, Tush and I did likewise. The kids, seeing our exaggerated movements, laughed and copied us, and we goose-stepped along, like a bizarre army of Fascists. We had gone perhaps twenty yards when a strange squeaking caused me to stop. There, waddling down the path as quickly as she could, her clothes crumpled and soiled, her hair a tangle of twigs, leaves and bark, was Mitzi.

'Wait for me, children, don't leave little Mitzi behind,' she panted.

When she finally reached us, she plonked herself down in a heap on the ground.

'I'll be needin' that wheelchair now, dearie,' she said to Tush, who was pushing Ross.

'The walk might do you good,' Tush said sweetly.

Mitzi blanched visibly.

It was the first time I had ever heard Tush refuse a child anything. I saw her exchange a knowing look with Lonnie, who was beaming from ear to ear. I felt another wave of resentment. Things were not working out how I – or Tristan, I felt sure – had planned.

When we got back on to the main road I stopped. I was in a foul mood and desperately worried about Tammy. I considered myself of no use to anyone.

'I'm going to stick around until I find Tammy,' I said to Susan, who was bringing up the rear of the group.

'Okay,' she said, unimpressed by the news.

'Look,' I said, knowing it needed to be said, 'you were right. The kids weren't ready for a trip like this. I fucked up.'

She sighed and patted me on the shoulder. 'Shane, I'm actually really surprised at how well most of them *did* do. We had a pretty good afternoon.'

I didn't know what to say.

'I'd bring them out again.' Susan trotted off after the others. When she had gone a short distance she called back: 'Tammy is up a tree just near where we were sitting. She climbed it about two minutes after we arrived. If I know her, you'll have to haul yourself up there too to get her down. Good luck.'

And then she was gone.

The woods were shady and cool as I retraced my steps. Somewhere in the distance a pigeon made a sound like an engine shuddering into life. I stood in the little clearing and felt like an alien invader. I walked slowly from one tree to another, peering upwards into the branches. I had to do the circuit three times, and was beginning to think Susan had been making fun of me – payback for my earlier grumpiness – before I spotted Tammy, a good thirty feet up among the branches. She was clinging to the trunk of the oak like a koala bear, and was completely motionless, as if she had somehow melded with the tree. My mind shot back to my conversation with Lonnie earlier that afternoon about the *krasnoludek* – the spirit of the wilderness. Tammy fitted the description. As I circled the base of the tree, trying to work out how to get up to her, I thought about how closely Lonnie seemed to identify with the children, while I was at constant loggerheads. Such thoughts were not helping me in my task, so I set them aside. For the moment.

I examined the branches and footholds I might use to get up to where she was perched, and was utterly befuddled as to how she could have scaled the ancient giant at all. I was certain I was going to have dire difficulty.

'Tammy,' I called. 'Tammy, it's Shane. The bus is going to be picking everyone up soon, so we have to go back to Little Scamps. Can you come down, honey?'

She didn't move. I wondered if she might be asleep, which filled me with even greater dread. If she woke up suddenly, she might easily fall and be killed or seriously injured.

I started to climb without thinking. I let my body do the job, trusting that pure instinct and physical memory would carry me unharmed to where I needed to go. As a child I had been an inveterate tree climber – most of the kids around the area where I grew up were – and a challenge of this sort would have been seen as a treat. From a lengthy career working with children I was acutely aware that the rules of adulthood quashed our delight in exploration. I just hoped my tree-climbing skills were not buried too deeply beneath layers of civilization.

As I moved I felt something come awake in my muscles – a sort of warmth and electricity. A trickle of sweat rolled down the small of my back. Was I enjoying myself?

Within a remarkably short time I was just below her – a tiny foot in a grubby off-white trainer dangled at my nose, and I could have touched her leg if I'd so wished. I worked my way around to the opposite side of the trunk and settled down more or less beside Tammy, but not too close.

She was not asleep. I could see clearly that her eyes were open, and her knuckles were white from the force of her grip on the bark of the tree. Tiny beads of sweat stood out on her forehead, which was stained green with moss and grime. She seemed almost catatonic.

'Tammy,' I whispered. 'You've given me quite a fright this afternoon, do you know that?'

No change in her.

'I thought you'd run away on me, and I was very worried about what I was going to tell your mam and dad. I don't think they'd be very pleased if I lost their little girl, would they?'

A twitch, right across her body, almost like a ripple on a pond.

'I'd feel pretty bad if I had to go on out to your house and tell them you'd taken off and I didn't know where you were. What do you reckon they'd say to me?'

Her eyes slid in my direction. The woods seemed to have become very still – even the wind had dropped. I could feel the weight of my body on the branch, the rough texture of the bole beneath my hands. I could smell pollen, soil and my own sweat. I reached out my hand to her. 'Will you let me take you down, Tammy love?'

She shook her head – two deliberate movements, left and right.

'I'm not mad, baby. I was a little bit before, when I was worried, and you might have heard me being cross with Milandra, but I'm not cross now.'

The shake again. She moved even closer into the tree – I hadn't thought it was possible for her to do so, but she managed it.

'Okay. Will we just sit here for a while, then?'

She nodded. I scooted around on my bum to get a bit more comfortable, supporting my back against an arching branch. I knew I should be talking to Tammy, reassuring her, trying to lure her down, but I didn't want to overload her. She had shown a huge leap of trust in responding to my overtures, and I sensed that overstepping the mark might make her clam up completely. So we rested, high above the ground.

I don't know how long we remained like that. I don't wear a watch. I had my mobile phone in my jacket pocket, and I dearly wanted to reach in and check the time to see if we had missed the bus, but I didn't want the child to think I was losing patience with her.

Time passed interminably. My arms ached from holding on, and I dared not look down – I'm not exactly afraid of heights but I have no great love of them, either. I was starting to get hungry, and worried about Millie. Dogs develop a natural sense of rhythm and routine. I thought it was probably a very long time past when I usually came home and fed her. But it was quite likely that Lonnie would anticipate how long I'd be, and call over to check on her.

That thought reminded me of the uncharitable feelings I had harboured towards my friend earlier, and I deliberately forced them aside again. Such a betrayal would have to be worked through, but just then was hardly the time.

The air slowly became cooler and the texture of the light changed from pale gold to a dusky grey. I glanced at Tammy

– she was gazing at me fixedly. 'I think it might start getting a little bit cold soon,' I said.

She shivered. She was wearing a thin T-shirt and a tatty pair of blue jeans that might have fitted her a year ago, but certainly didn't any more. She had little to protect her from the elements – I wondered how used she was to physical discomfort. Many children I had worked with in the past had become so acclimatized to cold, hunger, pain and distress that they shrugged off such sensations as part of their normal living conditions. Would Tammy register them, or ignore them completely?

'The bus will have gone by now, I'm sure, but there's a nice heater in my car, and I have the keys to Little Scamps right here in my pocket,' I said conversationally. 'I don't know about you, but I'm starting to get a little bit hungry. We could go in and have some supper before I drop you home. I could call your parents to let them know you were held up.'

Tammy shifted a little, seemingly not so confident in her position as she had previously been. I lapsed back into silence. I wondered what was going through her mind – she seemed stolidly determined to remain at her post, but then I had to question what had sent her up the tree in the first place. What was she running from? I remembered the first time I had met her. She had been clinging to a tree branch then, too, albeit one that was half in and half out of a lake. Why was she so drawn to trees?

The sun dipped further below the horizon somewhere beyond the treeline, and the light grew dimmer still. Behind me, I could hear the raucous clatter of hundreds of crows – mostly rooks, but I could make out the higher-pitched chatter of jackdaws, too, as they came in to roost for the night. The trees in the wood contained many nests, and I watched a shaggy black carrion crow settle on its spindly home in a neighbouring ash. That meant it had to be approaching eight o'clock.

I heard fluid dribbling – but it wasn't raining. I was puzzled for a second, then saw through the gloaming that liquid was trickling from the branch where Tammy was sitting – she had wet herself. Even in the semi-darkness, I could see that she was blushing ferociously, and indignant tears were welling in her eyes.

'You had an accident,' I said – it would have been pointless to ignore it.

She bit her lower lip and nodded. She was fighting hard not to cry, but the shame at what had happened was too much. A sob escaped, the first sound I had heard her make.

'Hey, don't cry,' I said, touching her gently on the arm. 'You didn't do anything wrong.'

The crying came full tilt then. Her whole body shook, racked with sobs and pain. I wanted to hold her, but was afraid of how she would react. So I hung there, like a strange bird, and patted her arm as she wept.

It seemed like for ever before the sobbing subsided, but Tammy still hiccuped and shuddered now and again. Darkness had settled like a cloak, and I knew that if we didn't move very soon we'd be stuck where we were for the rest of the night – it would be too dangerous to negotiate the climb.

'Tammy, we really have to go down to the ground now, okay?' I asked.

She nodded. When I reached out my arm she took it and swung over so she was resting against my chest with her arms about my neck.

'I'm going to climb down now, honey, and I'm going to go slowly and steadily, all right?' I told her. 'If you get afraid, just squeeze my neck and I'll stop for a moment. There's no harm in being scared.'

I took a quick glance down at my feet, and felt about until I had a good foothold. Then I started my descent.

I decided to use the same tactic for my downward journey as I had on the way up – and once again, it worked. Tammy dangled from me like a baby chimpanzee, seeming to trust me entirely. On one occasion my foot slipped and I swore loudly, but she never so much as whimpered, and the grip about my neck and shoulders never faltered for a second. Finally, after what felt like days, I set my boots on solid ground, every limb shaking from the effort, and whispered a silent prayer of thanks. I moved to lift Tammy down, but she wouldn't budge.

'You want me to carry you?' I asked her hoarsely, out of breath.

She nodded and wrapped her legs about my torso.

'Why don't I give you a piggy-back?' I asked.

She scurried round without giving me a chance to lift her, and sat on my shoulders, content.

'Okay.' I laughed. 'This is the last bus to Little Scamps from the Enchanted Wood tonight. I hope you have a ticket.'

Tammy grunted, which I assumed meant 'Yes'.

'Let's go, then.'

And off I went at a trot.

17

When we got back to the crèche I got the little girl a change of clothes from the spare sets we kept in case of emergencies, then made us both a ham and cheese omelette. When we had eaten, I dug out Tammy's file and found her mother's telephone number. It was a quarter to nine, a good five hours after Tammy usually arrived home, and I had a lot of explaining to do.

I sat in the office, watching the child as I waited for my call to be answered. She had taken up her position in the book corner, *Peter Rabbit* propped open in her lap. She was poring over the first page, her finger following one of the lines of text almost as if she was reading it. I smiled. Children let the adults around them know they're ready to read by mimicking reading behaviour – I had seen children I had worked with previously 'reading' to their dolls and teddy bears, reciting the stories their parents had read to them, or even making up new ones.

The call rang out. I tried again. And again. Kylie had not set up the message minder or voicemail on her mobile, so I couldn't even leave the news of Tammy's whereabouts on that. There was no number for Tammy's dad so I decided to just bring her home. I called Lonnie first.

'Lonnie, it's Shane.'

'So it is. You made it down out of the tree, I take it, or am I speaking to you from atop the canopy?'

'I'm back at Little Scamps, which you very well know because the number will have come up on your phone.'

'How can I help you?'

'Did you, by any chance, take a run by my place to check on Millie?'

'She's right here beside me. Would you like to say hello to her?'

I heaved an inner sigh of relief.

'No. She has a terrible phone manner. Next question: did anyone call Tammy's parents?'

'Of course they did. Su spoke to her mother.'

'Su?'

'Yes. She likes to be called Su.'

'I didn't know that.'

'You just don't communicate with your staff.'

I was starting to think he was right. I had been so taken up with sailing in and saving the day I had all but forgotten about establishing relationships with my fellow staff members. Lonnie, in his funny, self-effacing way, had won just about everyone over. Now that Tammy was safe and I was back in the relative safety of Little Scamps, I felt unspeakably ashamed of myself. 'Look, I know I've been a dork, Lonnie. I'm sorry, mate.'

'You don't deserve me. Or Tush and Su. Or Millie, for that matter.'

'I know. Look, what did Kylie say?'

'As I remember, Su reported that the bitch was already half cut and didn't give a fiddler's fuck. But I'm just paraphrasing.'

'Great. What am I supposed to do?'

There was silence for a moment. Then: 'You take her back

to her family, and we deal with it in the morning. Listen, Shane, Little Scamps is ultimately Tristan's responsibility. Maybe we should be talking to him about things. The situation in the place is . . . complicated, to say the least. I mean, let's face it, Tammy is not in a good place and Mitzi – that kid is fucked up, man.'

'Is that your professional assessment?'

'You're the guy with the letters after his name,' Lonnie shot back.

'I'm going to take this little one home, then, and I'll talk to you tomorrow. I assume it's okay if Millie sleeps over?'

'We're already in our jammies and are about to put on facemasks and do one another's hair.'

'I thought so.'

'All right, then – drive safely.'

'I will. And, Lonnie?'

'Yeah?'

'Thanks for everything today. You had my back, even though I didn't always have yours.'

'Heavy is the burden carried by the manager, my friend.'

'You can say that again.'

He didn't. He hung up.

18

I have not been blessed with a natural sense of direction, and even though I had been out to Tammy's home once before, I had not been driving and therefore hadn't been paying very close attention to the route the bus took. It therefore required several attempts, and some prompting from Tammy in the form of nods, grunts and pointing, to find my way to the odd little semicircle of houses adjoining its tidal swamp.

A half-moon hung amid scudding clouds in a sky pock-marked with glistening stars as I carried the tired child up to the front door. The wind hissed and whispered through the high reeds, and bats dive-bombed insects that clustered around a skeletal tree near the low wall.

By the coast, the air was even colder and heavy with mist, and I was anxious to get Tammy, tough nut though she was, out of the elements. She'd had enough adventures for one day – and I knew I had.

As I had feared, repeated knocking did not elicit a response. Through a glass panel beside the door I could see a light down what I presumed to be a hallway, but I was painfully aware that this did not mean anyone was at home. Kneeling down, Tammy still under my arm, I called in through the letterbox:

'Hello, it's Shane, from Little Scamps – I have Tammy here, and she really could do with getting to bed!'

Deeply frustrated and getting annoyed again, I hammered on the door. I heard the booming echo throughout the rooms, but it died away and we were left only with the whooshing of the wind through the bushes and whin trees behind us.

'I don't think anyone's in there, Tam,' I said at last, feeling utterly deflated.

The child shook her head in what might have been pity, hopped off my hip, reached down under the grimy doormat and took out a key. She handed it to me, motioning at the lock with a knowing nod.

'I don't think I should just go on in,' I said wearily. 'It's not my house.'

Tammy hopped up on to the plastic chair I had seen her use before, and held out her hand for the key.

I passed it to her.

A second later we were inside. I knew as soon as I was standing in the hallway that the house was not empty – it didn't have that edgy, uncomfortable feeling empty houses have. Tammy took my hand and led me down the hallway. The place smelt of cigarette smoke and cheap beer, like pubs used to before the smoking ban. Somewhere above us I could just make out the American punk band Green Day playing on tinny speakers – the song, I knew, was called 'Basket Case'. It seemed appropriate.

The room at the end of the hall was a kitchen and Kylie, Tammy's mother, was propped up at a rickety table, a can of lager in front of her, a cigarette burned down to the butt smouldering in her hand. She was asleep. Tammy patted her elbow and she stirred into awareness.

'I've brought Tammy home,' I said, when her eyes were focused on me.

'She's late,' Kylie said shakily. 'She missed her dinner.'

'I'm sorry about that,' I said. 'I fed her before we drove out.'

'I know you,' the woman said, her eyes narrowing. I recognized the expression – Tammy used it sometimes.

'Yes. We met out at the lake that day. I found Tammy in the water and brought her to you.'

'Oh – yeah. You want your towel back?'

I had to smile at that. 'No. Please accept it as a gift.'

She snorted. 'Needs a wash, anyway.'

There wasn't much to say to that. I tried to assess the situation: Kylie was drunk, but far from incoherent, and it seemed likely that Tammy would be going straight to bed anyway. I didn't think much could happen to her between the time I left and her arrival at Little Scamps the following morning. I decided that discretion was the better part of valour, and said my goodbyes.

'I'm going to head on,' I said. 'I'll see you tomorrow, Tammy. Apologies again, for keeping her so late today.'

Kylie dismissed me with a wave, and took a hefty gulp from her can. I left the two of them in the kitchen, and went back out to my car, feeling I might murder someone for a cigarette and wondering if I had made a bad day even worse by abandoning Tammy to the tender mercies of her mother.

I slept little that night, tossing and turning, the events and revelations of the day going round and round in my head as the hours dripped by. At five thirty, the sun already fully over the horizon, I showered and dressed and, a travel mug of coffee in hand, went out to the Austin.

I knew Tristan Fowler to be an early riser, and felt Lonnie's suggestion that I consult him was a sound one. His house was a half-hour drive away, and with no traffic on the road in the early morning I made it in twenty minutes.

As I had suspected, Tristan was out the back of his property, in the field where he kept his small collection of livestock. He had some chickens, a donkey and a couple of goats, and as I approached he was scattering seed for the clucking birds.

'You're up and about unusually early,' he said, when I leaned on the fence he had constructed to keep the animals in.

'Maybe I'll catch a worm,' I said.

'Maybe you will. How can I help you?'

'All is not well at Little Scamps,' I said. 'Actually, it's pretty shit.'

'Tell me.'

I explained about the events of the previous day, how badly things had gone, and how I felt I had only aggravated things. 'I'm going to be absolutely honest, Tristan,' I finished. 'I think I'm the wrong man for this job. You should have picked someone else, because it looks to me like I'm going to run that setting into the ground if I'm allowed to continue as I am.'

Tristan had finished with the hens and was pouring some feed from a bucket into a kind of trough for the goats.

'What are you saying, Shane?' he said. 'Do you want to throw your hat at it? Come back to Drumlin?'

'Yes!' I said. 'This is really not my area. I'm not good at it.'

'And what do I do with Lonnie? Will he come back with you?'

I sighed.

Tristan raised an eyebrow. 'Do I detect some dissent?'

'No. Yes. I'm not sure,' I said. 'I've been having some . . . issues, I'd suppose you'd call them.'

'Oh, yes?'

'Seeing Lonnie working at Little Scamps – and doing very well, might I add – hasn't been easy for me.'

105

'Why do you think that is?' Tristan asked.

'I don't know. It's weird.'

'How so?'

'I think I'm jealous.' I said. 'And maybe even a little resentful.'

Tristan nodded. He opened a small gate in the fence and came out to me. 'Lonnie Whitmore has made a transition not a lot of people make,' he said, walking slowly back towards the house. 'When he came to us, it was as a member of our client group. And while many might suggest that it is not politically correct to say so, the truth is that when we found him in that house, he *needed* to be a part of the client group. When I was certain he no longer needed help in that way, I began to give him responsibility and offer him tasks that suited a care worker at the unit, and I got him some training. I'm glad I did. I think he might be quite a talented worker.'

'He is,' I agreed glumly. 'He might be better than me.'

'Perhaps,' Tristan said. 'I know Lonnie's your friend, but you have to admit that, in the beginning, he was sort of a project for you.'

'That's a hard thing to say,' I said, feeling quite wretched.

'Indeed. But it's true,' Tristan said. 'Here was a case the like of which you had never seen before, and you were fascinated. I wondered, back at the beginning, if I should warn you off.'

'Why didn't you?'

Tristan pondered. 'I thought you might help one another.'

That knocked me for six. 'How so?'

'Loneliness runs both ways.'

We walked for a few minutes in silence.

'I mean it,' I said at last. 'I'm advising you leave Lonnie right where he is, and take me back to Drumlin. I'll be more use where I'm comfortable.'

'I'm not going to do that,' Tristan said.

'Why the hell not?' I asked. 'I'm handing you my resignation!'

'And I'm not accepting it,' Tristan said. 'You're finding the job much tougher than you expected. You've discovered that working alongside Lonnie and seeing him flourish and spread his wings is difficult too. Drumlin offers a protective bubble – the challenges of running a busy crèche can magnify existing problems.'

'That's for bloody sure,' I said sulkily.

'And have you considered that your jealousy or resentment is not necessarily just because Lonnie's doing well but because others are seeing him as you have – as a person – and you're protective of that? You and Lonnie have a bond. Sometimes it's intrusive to let other people in on that.'

'Yeah,' I said. 'Maybe.'

Tristan nodded sagely. 'Go into work today,' he said. 'I know you have plenty of ideas as to how you can sort out the issues in Little Scamps. Put a couple into action. Be proactive.'

'I've tried to be. I'm just alienating the staff and driving the kids to distraction.'

'Grow up, Shane,' Tristan said. 'Talk to your people. Ask them, don't tell them. If something you've tried doesn't work, adjust your technique. Look to the individual needs of the children, then try to respond to them. Come on, man, you've been doing this work a long time. You're getting a bit long in the tooth to be throwing temper tantrums.'

'Well, thanks for your sensitivity and understanding,' I said.

'Shane, I am very, very fond of you,' Tristan said, grabbing me in a bear hug. 'But sometimes, you can get just a little caught up in navel-gazing.'

'Thanks,' I said. 'I think.'

19

I arrived at the crèche early and spent an hour rearranging furniture in the main playroom. Everything had been taken out to facilitate the painting project, and for the past two days we had lived in the kitchen and the outdoor area. Now I felt we needed somewhere as a central operating point again. Anyway, we didn't require quite so much space to work on the murals – they didn't pose such a risk of paint-splatter and spillage.

On my way to work I had stopped at a twenty-four-hour supermarket and bought a couple of boxes of good breakfast cereal, some bread and a few cartons of juice. I also picked up some card, sticky tape and markers. I was ready for the day, and felt slightly better about myself – at least I was being proactive.

I explained my plans to Susan, Tush and Lonnie when they arrived, and they all agreed to give my ideas a go. While yesterday's débâcle had presented us with some challenges, they were not so great we hadn't been able to deal with them – Susan said I deserved a chance to redeem myself. And, of course, my latest scheme posed no threat to life or limb.

When the bus pulled up outside, the tables had been set for

breakfast. A large brightly coloured box with a slot in the top and a pile of brightly coloured cards sat in the middle among the plates of toast and jars of jam and marmalade.

The kids stood in their tight cluster when they came in, faced for the third day running with a major change. We had discussed as a staff group that we could not keep presenting them with such overwhelming upheavals – the stress would do more harm than good. I assured my colleagues that this would be the last. And I had a very good reason for it, anyway.

'Tammy gets no lunch, other than the one we provide,' I said, 'and she's not getting breakfast either. That means the first food she's consuming every day is around twelve thirty in the afternoon. How can we possibly expect her to learn anything when she doesn't know where the next meal is going to come from?'

'She knows we'll feed her,' Tush said. 'We always do.'

'Have you ever talked to her about it?' I asked. 'Reassured her?'

'No. I didn't want to embarrass her or anything.'

'I know you didn't,' I said. 'Look, you've been doing a great job – the food you're giving the child is probably what's keeping her going. I just think we need to formalize it a little. And it's not just Tammy who has problems with food.'

'Rufus,' Susan said. 'He steals food from the other kids now and again. And I know he comes in hungry a lot. Particularly on Mondays.'

'Then there's Mitzi,' Lonnie said. 'Although her difficulties with food are of a slightly different nature.'

I nodded.

'There's something to be said for teaching her a little bit about sharing,' Tush said.

'This could turn into an all-out massacre,' Lonnie said, looking at the laden table. 'Mitzi seems to feel it's her duty to cram as much into herself as she possibly can in as short a time as is humanly possible. And God help anyone who gets in the way.'

'I know,' I said. 'But Tammy and Rufus have a right not to be hungry. I don't think it's fair to single them out, and the only way to prevent that is to extend breakfast to everyone, regardless. I have no doubt in my mind that Mitzi eats a hearty meal before she gets on the bus in the morning, and in a way we're only compounding her obesity by presenting her with more food. But I don't know how to get around that, just now. Maybe we could think about it, and see if we can't come up with some ideas.'

We shepherded the children to the table and sat them down.

'From now on, we're going to start the day with break-fast,' Susan said. 'And while we eat, we'll have a chat about any news we have, about what we're going to do during the day, and anything else anyone would like to talk about.'

'Mealtime is all about coming together, talking and shar-ing,' Lonnie said. 'So – who would like cereal?'

To my delight the children took to the idea enthusiastic-ally. Soon we were all happily eating, there was an easy hum of conversation, nobody was punching or puking on anyone else and I waited for somebody to notice the second part of my plan. It didn't take long. Gus, his mouth full of cornflakes, suddenly pointed with his spoon at the gaudily decorated cardboard box with its accompanying cards.

'What's dat ting dere?'

'Ah, that's something very special,' I said, winking at him. 'I think you're going to like it.'

'Whassit for?' Ross asked, standing up and jabbing at the item with a crutch, thumping Tammy's head accidentally as he did so.

'Let Shane explain,' Susan said, carefully manoeuvring Ross's appendage back down and shushing Tammy, who was looking at her unwitting attacker with balled fists.

'All right, then,' I said. 'Everyone needs to listen to this because it affects all of you. That box is what I call a "Kindness Box".'

'A what?' Milandra said. 'That sure sounds like a goddam stupid pussy box to me!'

'What does it do?' Gilbert asked. 'Is it a magic box?'

'Maybe there is kindness inside it,' Mitzi said, as Tush wrestled a jar of jam from her hand – she had been scooping the contents out with her fingers and noisily sucking them clean.

'Mitzi's sort of right,' I said. 'There will be kindness inside it, and we are going to put it there.'

That caused some bewilderment, which was expressed in the children's chatter: what could Shane possibly mean? Could something like kindness be put in a cardboard box? I decided that the subject was worth exploring, so I raised my hand.

'All right, all right,' I called, trying to be heard above the din. 'One person at a time, please. I want to hear what everybody has to say.'

Despite my best efforts, this caused an even greater clamour, as every child in the group (even those who were technically non-verbal) strove to be the first person to speak. I was at a complete loss as to how to get any kind of control without resorting to all-out shouting. Once again, Lonnie rescued me. He had come prepared, and as the group descended into its by now familiar chaos, he produced an old metal tray from beneath the table and struck it with a spoon. It made a fine old noise. Every mouth in the room closed, and every head in the room turned to look at him.

Lonnie stopped. 'When everyone talks together, that's sort of what it sounds like to me,' he said, giving another couple of raps on the tray. Arga put her hands over her ears. 'It's not a nice sound, is it, Arga?' Lonnie asked, rolling her *r* perfectly. 'I bet you don't like it either, Jeff, do you?' Jeffrey shook his head. 'I think it would be much kinder to everyone if I didn't make this sound again. Wouldn't you all say?' Nods came from almost all quarters. Milandra and Mitzi were the two withholders of agreement. I wondered if they actually enjoyed discord so much that they had liked Lonnie's clanging. Lonnie, however, chose to ignore them and talk to the rest of the gang. 'If you think about it, isn't it so much better if we take it in turns to talk? Then everyone gets heard and understood.'

There were murmurs of agreement.

'Thank you, Lonnie,' I said. 'Now, I think Mitzi was speaking.'

'Yes, you should all listen to me, children,' Mitzi gushed.

'What did you want to say about the Kindness Box?' Tush said.

'I think it's a good idea,' she said. 'I could go and take kindness any time I wanted. All for me.'

'But can you put kindness in a box like that?' Susan asked.

Rufus put his hand up timidly.

'Go ahead, Ru.' She nodded at him.

'Kindness is doing something nice for somebody else,' he said. 'Like having a nice breakfast for us when we come in. That's kind.'

I'm not ashamed to admit that I felt a warm glow. It's one of the things I love about child- and social-care work: just when you think you've messed up badly, something small happens to lift you off the ground again. That morning, I needed all the back-patting I could get.

'Yes, it is,' Susan said, smiling at me. 'So, how do you think we might put something like that in the box?'

'Maybe ideas of how we could be kind to one another,' Ross said.

'Mmm,' Lonnie agreed. 'But see, if I told you how to be kind to me, gave you ideas for things I liked – well, is that as good as when you think things up yourself?'

Arga whispered something to Lonnie, who listened carefully and nodded.

'Arga says that being kind is when you do something for someone else without being asked to do it,' he shared with the group.

'Will I tell you how the Kindness Box works?' I asked everyone.

I'd stolen the idea wholesale from another childcare worker and writer, the brilliant Torey Hayden. I have adapted it a little bit to suit Irish children (Torey was working in America when she invented the concept), but the principle is exactly the same.

'Here's the deal,' I said. 'I'm going to be watching very carefully from now on to see how kind you all are to each other. Every time I see somebody doing something kind for another person, I'm going to write down what I see and put it in this box. But I know that you're all very kind people, and there will be lots and lots of kind things going on, so I'm going to need your help. If *you* see one of the group being kind, I want you to come and tell me or Lonnie or Sue or Tush. I know some of you can write a little, and if you want to write down what you see, well, you do that and put it in the box, or if you need help, any of us will give you a hand to write down your little bit of kindness.'

'We're going to fill this old box right up with kindness,' Tush added.

'Every day we'll open the box before we go home and see what's in there,' I said. 'Every person who has some kindness in the box gets a prize.'

'Yeah!'

'Cool!'

'I'm gonna put loads of things in that box!'

Expressions of excitement and approval abounded. I held up my hand again. The chatter continued. Lonnie picked up the tray. Silence. He didn't even have to hit it.

'Very good,' I said. 'Now, I'm really pleased you like the idea of the Kindness Box, but there's just one rule and it's an important one.'

All faces were rapt and attentive. I couldn't help smiling. The box was working its magic already, and not one single message had been put in there yet.

'The rule is this,' I said. 'No one can put in an act of kindness they did themselves.'

'What?' Gus asked, puzzled.

'You can only put in kind things *other people did*,' Lonnie clarified.

There were moans and groans from one end of the table to the other.

'That's the rule,' I said. 'The thing is, everyone is going to have to be really kind to their friends to make sure they get into the box.'

'Yeah,' Ross grumbled. 'Now I'm gonna have to be *really* nice to everyone.'

After the previous day's disastrous events, I was fascinated to see how this new development would work. I hoped we had hit on something that would harness the spirit I knew these youngsters had buried deep inside – and that maybe some of that kindness might infect me, too.

20

At three o'clock that afternoon I was in the office sifting through a mountain of notes the staff, and indeed some of the children, had written and placed in the Kindness Box – Tush had started referring to it midway through the morning as 'the KB' and it had stuck. I was utterly amazed at what had happened in Little Scamps that day. The box had proved powerful when I'd used it previously, but I'd held out no great hope for these children. I figured it might keep them going for perhaps a morning before they got bored and returned to all-out aggression. I had suspected some of them might behave themselves when one of the adults was close by, but continue their reign of terror when they thought no one was looking.

To my absolute shock, none of these things occurred. Instead, almost all of the kids went out of their way to outdo one another in acts of generosity, thoughtfulness and decency. I picked up a page at random. Written in Lonnie's precise hand I read: *Rufus, when he put his fire engine away so Ross didn't trip on it – Gus.* I picked up another. *I saw Tammy give the football to Julie so she could have a turn – Arga.* Another: *Jeffrey could have catched Milandra when we was playing chase, but he letted her go so she could still play.* It went on and on. There were at least forty messages. Things had gone off without a hitch. Almost.

For it to work, every child had to be represented in the KB, but this had been a far more challenging proposal than any of us had suspected. While kind acts were coming at Tush, Susan, Lonnie and me thick and fast, there were two individuals who doggedly refused to participate in all this unexpected goodwill: Milandra and Mitzi.

Milandra wasted no time in declaring to all and sundry that she was not going to be kind to no girly-arsed kids, and no one had better try being nice to her either so they could get some shitty prize. This did not dissuade her compatriots, as the notes had shown (although I did wonder if Jeffrey had decided not to catch her out of fear rather than any desire to do her a good turn), and I'd had to be extremely observant to spot any actions that might be suitable for entry in the KB. In the end, I settled on: *Milandra went a whole ten minutes without saying a rude word.* In fact, it was closer to eight, but I didn't think rounding the figure up would do any harm.

Mitzi proved even more difficult. She had no argument with kindness in general, but believed all such activity should be directed in her favour – she had no intention of doing anything that benefited anyone else. This meant that her food snatching, sneak bullying and all-round nastiness continued unabated, accompanied, as usual, with a cloying smile. Sporadic monitoring throughout the day produced not one eye-witness account of her doing anything that came within an ass's roar of basic human courtesy, let alone kindness. Hers was the only name not in the box. I picked up a blank card and a pen. I had to put something in that identified (and, hopefully, encouraged) some kindness in Mitzi. I chewed the end of the Biro, watching her through

116

the glass window. She was sitting at the very far end of the room, an old teddy bear lying face down across her knees. Everyone else was at the table, drawing pictures of Peter Rabbit, to be copied on to the wall in mural form. Mitzi had refused to join them, looking for someone to carry her over – a demand that was ignored. As I watched, she picked up the bear, looked at it with a dour expression, then gripped it firmly around the neck, clearly intending to rip its head off.

I knew from watching the children play that this worthy old bear was a particular favourite. Other toys had been torn, smashed or mangled but it had somehow been spared the worst viciousness. My heart dropped as Mitzi considered her act of butchery. A toy that managed to be so loved in a place like Little Scamps deserved better.

We sat there, Mitzi and I, she at one end of the room, me at the other, each locked in our private deliberations. Finally, as if she simply decided it wasn't worth it, Mitzi tossed the bear aside, a look of disgust on her face, and began to pick her nose. Laughing to myself, I took up my pen again: *Mitzi: for deciding not to tear Old Man Bear's head off.*

I didn't know if this was a true act of kindness or an expression of laziness. And for once I didn't care.

It wasn't all sweetness and light that day. Mitzi's desire to continue with her ill will seemed, at some points, almost like a vendetta, and even the children tired of it. I came into the entrance hall, a short passageway between the front door and the main activity room, at around eleven thirty to find Tammy sitting on the floor, Gilbert wrapped in her arms, sobbing loudly.

'Hey, what happened?' I asked, kneeling down beside them.

Tammy, of course, was silent. Gilbert finally blurted out: 'Mitzi hurted me.'

I could see livid marks on his arm, the imprint of someone's teeth. Mitzi, I knew, was an inveterate biter. 'Okay, champ,' I said, rubbing his back. 'I think you'll survive. It was a very mean thing to do, though, wasn't it?'

Tammy continued to cuddle him, and when they finally returned to the group, she watched Mitzi very closely.

After lunch we had planned to go for a walk up the village to a little stream to fish for frog-spawn. There was a pond in a field behind the crèche, and Ross thought it would be cool if we had some tadpoles in it. The village slanted upwards in a sort of shallow hill, and Mitzi refused to walk.

'You can take me in the wheelchair, possum,' she whimpered at me. 'I would love to come, but I cannot walk.'

I went to get the chair, only to find Tammy sitting in it, swinging her legs extravagantly. She wasn't smiling – in all my time with her, I never saw her smile – but there was a look of something on her face. Triumph, perhaps?

'Out you get, Tamster,' I said. 'I need the wheelchair for Mitzi.'

Tammy slowly slid out of the chair and followed me as I wheeled it across the room to where Mitzi was sitting on the floor, near the Messy Area. I stopped halfway.

'We have a problem,' I said. 'The tyres are flat.'

'Then blow them up, precious,' Mitzi said.

'I can't,' I said. 'The petrol station across the road doesn't have a tube that fits these tyres.'

Tammy watched us both expectantly.

'Look, it's not far, Mitzi,' I said. 'You're going to have to walk. You can take breaks if you need them.'

I will not describe the temper tantrum that followed. Suffice it to say that Mitzi *did* walk. Eventually.

When she finally waddled out of the door, swearing under her breath, I knelt down in front of Tammy. 'How'd you do it?' I asked her.

She surveyed me with huge eyes.

'I know you let the air out of the tyres,' I said. 'I'm not mad. How'd you do it?'

Tammy opened her hand. There was a rusty nail in it – she must have used it to depress the nozzle on the air fitting.

'You'd better let me have that,' I said. 'If you cut yourself on it, you'll get blood poisoning.'

She handed it over, and we went to look for frog-spawn. Tammy had paid Mitzi back – she was not, it seemed, someone to cross.

21

The kids were making their way out to the bus, all sucking red-and-white-striped sugar-free dentist-approved environmentally friendly lollipops, their prizes for so many unsolicited acts of goodwill. Susan, Tush, Lonnie and I were seated about the table, idiotic grins on our faces.

'It's only one day,' I said. 'Don't forget that. Yesterday was awful.'

'I don't care,' Susan said. 'Those kids behaved like human beings today, for the first time. It wasn't just that nobody ended up in hospital – they were actually nice to be around.'

'I gave Gus a tissue to wipe his nose this afternoon, and he said, "Thank you".' Tush burst into what might have been laughter or tears – it was impossible to tell.

'All because of a fucking cardboard box,' Susan said.

'Don't diss the box,' Lonnie said, only half joking. 'It'll hear you.'

I was about to start tidying up the last few bits of art material when the door opened and a woman I recognized as Rufus's mother came in.

'I needs to speak to him,' she said, motioning at me with a nod.

Without a word the others took themselves off to various far-flung corners of the room so we could talk.

'Hello, Mrs Ward,' I said, thinking my visit must have had a positive effect after all, and she had come to volunteer to help. 'Would you like some tea?'

The woman looked as though she was about to faint from nerves. She glanced unhappily at Lonnie and the women, but followed me towards the table.

'No, thank you. I needs to talk to ye about my Rufus.'

I motioned at a chair and sat down myself. 'All right. How can I help you?'

'He's got some quare ideas these last days. Strange notions.'

I nodded. 'Okay – could you be a little bit more specific?'

Mrs Ward was struggling to express herself. 'I had to slap him last night, and my husband gave him a right hidin'. He said it was you told him to do it.'

'To do what, Mrs Ward? I want to be of assistance, but I really don't understand.' I was at a loss. Rufus had been very well behaved, and had shown no signs of being upset or angry.

'The rabbits,' the woman said, pointing at a picture of Peter Rabbit we had put on the wall.

'Yeah, we're sort of working on a project at the moment,' I said. 'Rufus seems to be very interested in it. He's been asking questions, and doing lots of artwork . . .'

'He says the rabbits are his friends,' Mrs Ward said, her voice trembling. 'Talkin' and playin' games. He says we should mind them. He wouldn't go lampin' with his da. And he wouldn't eat his dinner, even though I told him there was no rabbit in it.'

My stomach lurched. I had not expected this. Despite the easy availability of rabbit in Ireland, it is rarely used as a food source now. I didn't think my Beatrix Potter project would have a negative impact on anyone's dietary habits. But, of course, for many families among the travelling community, rabbit was still a staple.

'Oh, God, I'm sorry,' I said. 'I never told him not to eat rabbit . . .' But I knew how what I *had* said would have been interpreted by the children.

'His da is talkin' about not lettin' him come here no more,' Mrs Ward said. 'What can I do? I know the lad needs to come, but if he don't shape up . . .'

'I'll talk to him – I promise,' I said, my mind reeling. 'He doesn't mean any harm. He's actually doing what he thinks is right.'

Mrs Ward looked at me as if I had three heads. 'Sure that ain't for him to decide,' she said. 'We're his parents, me and John Joe. We tell him wha's right.'

I nodded. 'Don't punish him, please,' I implored. 'I'll make certain you have no further difficulty in getting him to eat or do any of his other chores. He's a good kid – he learns fast.'

She paused, surprised at that statement.

'Do he?'

'He does. I think he's very bright.'

It was as if she suddenly grew six inches, and years dropped away from her face. 'My boy?'

'Rufus, yes. He's so interested in everything we do here, and he already has some literacy skills. Did you know that?'

This was met by a blank expression.

'Um . . . reading . . . writing . . .' I said. To illustrate my point, I went over to the library corner and picked up the KB. It took me around thirty seconds to find one of Rufus's notes. I pushed it over to her, assuming that, if Rufus could already read a little, she could too – some travellers have been ill served by the education system.

'*Cos Ross shared his cake with me,*' Mrs Ward read haltingly. '*Rufus.*'

'We're trying to teach the children about kindness,' I explained, showing her the box and some of the other notes.

It was as if the box worked its magic all over again. Mrs Ward went through the notes with me, laughing and chatting, asking how Rufus interacted with the other children, and marvelling at the notes – there were many – that commented on *his* kindness to others. I felt myself relax: the stress and anxiety this woman had exuded when she walked into the room had had little, if anything, to do with me or Little Scamps. I imagined there was probably a history of unpleasantness between Mrs Ward and people who worked in classrooms. To try and explain that this was a crèche, not a school, would have been pointless. I was just delighted I had accidentally found some common ground with her – a shared interest in her son.

She stood up to leave, her face still lit by a smile.

'I'll make sure Rufus understands about the rabbits,' I said, offering my hand, which she shook.

'All right, then,' she said.

She stopped at the door. 'You said before you wanted parents to come in and help from time to time.'

'We do. I mean, that would be great if you or your husband . . .'

'He wouldn't come near the place!'

'Well, you then . . .'

She pushed the door wide. 'Maybe I will,' she said. 'The odd time, like.'

And she was gone. I wanted to whoop and cheer, but I wasn't sure if I had actually done anything to bring about such a positive change, so I settled for silently waving my fist in the air in victory.

Tristan Fowler had been right: by setting aside my self-consciousness and focusing on the job, I had taken some real steps forward. It was to be the first of several occasions during my time in Little Scamps where his guidance proved invaluable.

Fiona Thomson, the social worker who had taken over with Tammy when Imelda Gibb had moved on, sat opposite me in a café in town. She was a petite redhead with a garish fashion sense and a keen sense of humour. I liked her immediately.

'How long did you work with the family?' I asked, when we had coffee and a slice of cake in front of us.

'About a year and a half, all told,' Fiona said.

'Why'd you get taken off the case?' I asked.

'Tammy was placed in a crèche, and the powers that be felt Dale and Kylie could manage on their own.'

'What did you think?'

Fiona was maybe thirty years old, not exactly pretty but with a warm, intelligent face, sprinkled with freckles.

'I thought they were a very, very messed-up family. You've read the report?'

'I used to do child protection,' I said. 'I know that reports like that just point out the main issues but that the devil is in the detail.'

'Yes indeed.'

'Fill me in,' I said.

'Jesus, how long have you got?'

'As long as I need,' I said.

'When I started out with Kylie and Dale, Tammy was still very little. The initial reason for my doing home visits was to offer a listening ear to Kylie, because the public-health nurse seemed to feel she was depressed. I'd done that kind of work before, and I have a nursing background.'

'How'd it go?'

'Well, it was easy to see how the PHN might have thought Kylie was depressed. But I have to tell you, I'm not so sure she was.'

'She had rejected Tammy, though, hadn't she?' I asked. 'Dale was doing everything.'

'Yes. And he was glad to,' Fiona said, taking a bite of chocolate cake and chasing it with a sip of coffee. 'It was like he was so delighted to have this little thing, his flesh and blood, that he didn't *want* Kylie to take any responsibility. He'd say, "Kylie ain't the motherin' sort." I mean, how could she behave any differently? On the rare occasion she actually did pick Tammy up, the child would screech and Dale would step in right away, a satisfied grin on his face. It was sickening to watch.'

'What did you do?'

'Well, Dale wasn't working, but he did go out occasionally. I suppose you're aware of his and Kylie's love of booze?'

'It was one of the first things I noticed about them.'

'Well, he goes to this shitty pub not far from where they live. When he went for his thrice-weekly piss-up session, I'd try and get Kylie to bond with the child. It was an uphill struggle. I wish I could say otherwise, but the woman just wasn't interested. There was nothing there. Tammy was getting on for six months by then, and I was starting to despair of ever effecting even the most superficial relationship between the pair of them.'

'And did you?' I asked. 'From what I've seen, they're not exactly bosom buddies now.'

'Well, it was kind of a matter of necessity,' Fiona said. 'Things went pear shaped between Tammy and Dale.'

'Wasn't Tammy still a baby?' I asked, aghast.

'She was. You see, it started to become obvious that things weren't right with her.'

'Okay,' I said. 'Can you be very specific about that? When, precisely, did you notice something was up with her?'

Fiona shook her head. 'It's hard to be specific. It was gradual. There were some things she just shot ahead at developmentally. She walked very early – she was nearly running by the time she was eight months old – and was climbing well before a year. She had wonderful manual dexterity – she could use a pencil perfectly long before she should have done, and I swear to you, I believe she knew her colours and a lot of letters and numbers. It was the way she responded to them.'

'But in all the time you were with her, she never spoke,' I said. 'Even though she seemed so bright.'

'That was the real problem,' Fiona said. 'Dale put hours into trying to get her to talk. He read to her, sang her songs, played games. Nothing. She just wasn't having any of it. Now, she lapped up the attention, and seemed to relish all the activities – it wasn't that she was unhappy, not then. It was just like she'd decided she wasn't ready to speak yet, and nothing was going to make her until she was good and ready.'

'But she's still not speaking,' I said. 'Not only is she not speaking, she's not making any effort to communicate with anyone. Do you know that I have never seen that child smile?'

'Dale brought her to the doctor when she was two,' Fiona said. 'The doctor put it to him that the little girl might be disabled in some way – maybe autistic or intellectually delayed.'

'How'd he take it?' I asked, already knowing the answer.

'Not well. I was there when he got home. He screamed and ranted, hit Kylie, walloped Tammy, said that no blood of his would be a retard. He suggested that Kylie might have been putting it about a bit – that Tammy was some other bloke's baby.'

'Harsh,' I said, 'though not impossible, I suppose.'

'Not helpful, either,' Fiona said. 'He washed his hands of her. In the time I was there – and it was not long after that because she was placed in the playschool – he never spoke to her again. And she never looked at him either. It was like they were dead to each other.'

'And Kylie?'

'Bizarrely the whole kerfuffle seemed to bring something alive in her. She didn't exactly become Mother of the Year, but she did start to pay a bit more attention to Tammy. I told the senior social worker that I was still needed in that house, but you know what child-protection caseloads are like. They couldn't spare me on a case that was then, officially, under the jurisdiction of the intellectual-disability department.'

We paused for a few moments in companionable silence. The cake was gone, and we sipped what was left of our coffee.

'Tammy is completely shut down,' I said to Fiona at last. 'If I'm to help her at all, I need to get through the pretty thick walls she's constructed, and I simply do not know how.'

'Wish I could help,' she said, smiling sadly. 'I'd guess that her father might be your best asset, but I doubt he'll ever get over the shock of finding out his little princess isn't perfect.'

I thought about that one. 'Or maybe he needs to learn that she *is* perfect,' I said.

'Good luck with that,' Fiona said.

22

Saturday afternoon. It was a warm day and I was preheating the oven to bake so the kitchen windows were open. Mississippi Fred McDowell was playing on the stereo and I had just finished setting out the cake ingredients. Milandra was five on Monday, and I have a very simple policy when working in childcare settings: no one's birthday slips by without a fuss being made, not even those of people who threaten to punch anyone who mentions the celebration of their nativity.

Lonnie had agreed to come over to help with the baking, an offer that was something of a double-edged sword. My friend was a frightening experimental cook, who simply refused to take direction, though he was remarkably enthusiastic and had an insatiable appetite for knowledge of any kind. He seemed to feel that his bizarre forays into the culinary arts were all for the good of gastronomic science so I generally tolerated the small explosions, oddly coloured smoke and difficult-to-remove crusts that were left on my pans when he was done. He was, after all, fun to have around, so I wrote off the damage as a sacrifice I would just have to make.

Millie yawned loudly at my feet. She had developed a

talent for getting in the way whenever I tried to move about the kitchen, able to time her movements to coincide exactly with my own: when I chose to cross from the cooker to the sink, there she would be, sprawled right across the room. I would step over her, check the oven, then make a move for the fridge – and, as if by magic, my dog would now be pressed tight against its door, gazing at me innocently. If Millie hadn't been quite as daft as she was, I'd have been convinced she was doing it to annoy me.

'Hello, the house!' Lonnie called, from somewhere below the kitchen window. I turned from pondering the evil machinations of my angelic-looking greyhound to see Tush's face smiling prettily in at me from the garden.

'Oh, hello,' I said, heading for the door to let them in. 'I wasn't expecting you.'

'I didn't think you'd mind,' Lonnie said, shuffling in behind her. 'Tush called over to go for a stroll, and I'd forgotten I'd agreed to babysit you for the afternoon, so I figured she could come along and lend a hand.'

'The more the merrier,' I said.

It was just as well Tush had joined us for it became clear almost immediately that baking a cake for Milandra was not going to be straightforward.

'Well, I figured we'd go for chocolate cake,' I said, when we were gathered around my worktop. 'Everyone likes chocolate, after all.'

'Everyone except Milandra,' Tush said. 'She hates it.'

'What?' I asked, appalled. 'How could she hate chocolate?'

I looked ruefully at the dark chocolate I had bought for the cake.

Lonnie was standing on a chair, riffling through one of my cupboards. 'Marmite?' he said, holding up a large jar. 'How about a Marmite cake?'

Tush chewed her lower lip, clearly perplexed. 'I don't think she'd like that either,' she said. 'Actually, I don't think anyone likes Marmite.'

'Does it seem reasonable I would have it in my larder if I didn't?' I said.

Tush took the jar from Lonnie, who returned to foraging. 'What's in Marmite, anyway?'

'It's a yeast extract,' I said, returning my attention to the much more sensible ingredients I had before me. 'Some sort of by-product of the brewing process.'

'Okay,' Lonnie said, from the depths of the press. 'I've got some pickled gherkins and an unopened jar of salad cream. Don't either of you tell me we can't do something with those!'

An hour later we were no further forward. Tush admitted she had never heard Milandra express a fondness for cakes of any sort. I wondered aloud if she had been raised on Nigerian desserts, and we spent another hour researching African food online. Other than fruit, the Nigerian diet seemed to focus almost exclusively on the savoury end of the gourmet spectrum. I did, however, come across a recipe for a very simple dish called Colour Cake, which seemed to be a basic Madeira mix with food colouring added. I was more or less set on this when Tush threw another spanner in the works.

'Of course,' she said, 'the kids are all so picky and difficult when it comes to eating, you'll never keep everyone happy.'

'What do you mean?' I asked, closing the laptop. 'I want to make a cake, not force them to eat broccoli.'

'I know. I'm just pointing out that even very simple things can turn into an episode with our little angels.'

I sat back, the urge for a cigarette inserting itself into my skull like a drill.

'Maybe if we made some small cakes with the Marmite and the gherkins in them . . .' Lonnie said hopefully. 'So the kids could just try them.'

I sat up suddenly.

'That's it,' I said. 'We'll do a cupcake mountain.'

'A what?' Tush asked.

'A cake that's made up of lots of different fairy cakes. We can do half a dozen different flavours – or more, if you like.'

'That way, everyone will find something they like,' Tush said, seeing where I was going with the idea.

'Exactly,' I said. 'We can do some of these Colour Cakes, but some chocolate, some vanilla, some strawberry . . .'

'Some Marmite, some sardine . . .' Lonnie said. I wasn't sure he was joking.

As it turned out, he wasn't. We did the cakes in three batches, as my oven had only two shelves. In one consignment Lonnie produced his off-the-wall creations. When they came out of the oven, they smelt distressingly good, and looked just like ordinary cakes. Lonnie proudly pointed out marmalade and pickle, anchovy and caper, Marmite (even Lonnie had to admit that he could not come up with a flavour combination that worked on that one, so had decided to allow the central ingredient to speak for itself), and Nutella with onion. Tush and I nodded approvingly, and went back to decorating the others with butter icing, hundreds and thousands and chocolate sprinkles. The finished articles looked delicious, so I boxed them up and set them aside for Monday's festivities.

When Tush had gone, Lonnie and I took Millie for a walk in the fading evening light.

'You and Tush getting friendly, mate?' I asked, as we strolled through the village.

'I suppose we are,' he said. 'It was her idea to meet up.'

'Did you think that maybe she hadn't intended to spend the afternoon with me too?'

Lonnie shrugged. 'Why not? You're my friend.'

'Yeah, and I can't help but wonder if Tush hadn't planned on you and she getting to . . . uh . . . to know one another better. Do you get what I'm saying?'

'Yeah, well, of course . . .' Lonnie spluttered. 'Actually, no. I haven't a clue what you're talking about.'

We climbed a gate and followed the by now galloping Millie across a field peppered with bluebells.

'I'm saying I think Tush likes you.'

'Well, I surely like her. Don't you?'

'Of course I fucking do, Lonnie, but I think she *likes* you.'

'You've just said that.'

I stopped and looked him dead in the eye. 'I think she wants to be your girlfriend. And if you try to dodge that by pretending to be stupider than you actually are, I'll strangle you and leave you for the buzzards.'

Lonnie snorted and continued to walk after the dog – a vague black smudge at the other end of the field. 'Don't be daft. Why would Tush want to be with a creature like me?'

'I don't know,' I said. 'I'm as puzzled about that as you are. But I suppose it might have something to do with the fact that she thinks you're smart and funny and confident and, Christ, maybe even a bit good looking.'

'Shag off,' Lonnie said. 'You're not making sense.'

'Why not?'

'Because Tush is beautiful, that's why.'

'And a beautiful girl could never be even slightly interested in Lonnie Whitmore?' I shot back.

132

'A beautiful girl is never going to be attracted to a dwarf,' he said.

'I gotta tell you, Lonnie, I think you're wrong,' I said. 'Tush is into you, and if you'd just open up, you might see I'm on the money.'

23

Sonya Kitchell was stick thin with long, Joni Mitchell-style straight ash-blond hair hanging halfway down her back. She was dressed in flared blue jeans and a mustard yellow woollen jumper. It was eight in the morning, and I knew the children she worked with in her crèche, Tiny Flowers, would be arriving within the next half-hour.

'I'm not sure I should be talking to you at all,' Sonya said, squinting at me over the top of her mug of camomile tea.

'A simple phone call would have verified who I am,' I said. 'And I'm not asking for anything terribly confidential or sensitive. I'm simply trying to establish how Tammy ended up in the state she's in now – chart the trajectory of her behaviour, if you like. I thought you might be able to help.'

'It's not really normal for a man to work in a playschool.' Sonya sniffed.

'What's normal got to do with anything?' I asked, trying to sound light and conversational, even though she was beginning to annoy me. 'Look, Sonya, we're on the same side here. I want to help this little girl. Do you want to help me do that? Because I can go and you need never see me again. I can request a full written report through Social Services, which will take up much more of your time. You don't want to do it that way any more than I do.'

'S'pose not,' she said. 'What do you want to know?'

'Tammy was around two years old when she started coming to Tiny Flowers,' I said. 'According to her file, her placement here was requested by Child Services. I've been told that in many ways Tammy was very bright, maybe even a bit advanced for her age, except in terms of speech. What was her behaviour like when she found herself among other children?'

'Initially she was very distant,' Sonya said. 'But that is hardly unusual when children first come to an early-years setting. I thought she'd settle down in a day or so.'

'Did she?'

'No. She resisted every attempt my staff and I made to involve her. All she wanted to do was perch in the book corner and flick through the books. When we brought her back out to the group she at first ran away, then turned on the other children. She spent a lot of time sitting in the time-out chair, let me tell you.'

'What did you do to try and manage her behaviour?'

'Time out.'

'Anything else?'

'That's the method we use here.'

I nodded. 'Did you see any improvement?'

'She is an incorrigibly ill-mannered little girl. Her behaviour proved too disruptive for the other children. And her aggression became far more pronounced. She put little Luke Hancock in the hospital – broke his nose! I can't have that in Tiny Flowers. That's not what we're about.'

'Do you have any thoughts on what might be causing Tammy's anger?' I asked. 'I mean, it's not what you'd call standard behaviour for a child of her age.'

'Her parents refused to come in and talk to me about it,' Sonya said. 'I did talk to Fiona, the social worker, on one occasion, but she just said there were some problems within the family. It's not my job to investigate such matters. I asked for Tammy to be moved – and, thankfully, she was in the end.'

I grinned, although I felt no real warmth for Sonya. I could understand that Tammy had made her life quite unpleasant for a while, but I felt she had done very little to help the child. 'Anything else that might help?' I asked.

'That little girl belongs in an institution,' Sonya said. 'I'm afraid I must ask you to trot along now. I think I hear the bus outside.'

'Well, thanks for your time,' I said.

I had a picture now, at least, of where Tammy had come from. I just wasn't sure it helped me very much.

Tammy and Arga were fighting like tiny Tasmanian devils. The only thing I could think to do was to scoop the pair of them up and carry them away from the rest of the children – who were not behaving much better that morning: the weekend seemed to have killed some of their ardour for the KB. In fact, the atmosphere in Little Scamps that morning was not one bit pleasant – I feared we were balanced on a knife-edge, but clung to the belief that Milandra's impending party might set things back on track.

I hauled the two scuffling children down to the reading area, where we had a circle of beanbags, and unceremoniously dumped them on the large, soft cushions. Arga immediately went for Tammy with her hands bared like claws, and I was forced to get between the pair, receiving a nasty scratch across my forehead for my trouble.

'Okay, you two,' I said, my voice firm. 'That is absolutely enough.'

Tammy made a kind of hissing sound and tried to barge past me to get at her antagonist, and Arga screeched something in rapid Polish: '*Wyrwę sobie oczy, ty suko!*'

'I'll tear out your eyes, you bitch,' Lonnie called, from the dress-up corner, where Mitzi was stationed, trying on outfits for the party – she'd said she wanted to look beautiful, and who were we to argue?

'I don't want you talking like that, Arga,' I said.

She snarled at me like a wild dog, then folded her arms in a huge sulk.

'Look at the pair of you,' I said, sitting down between them. 'We've got a party coming up later on. You don't want to be fighting for that, do you?'

Tammy looked at me, wide eyed. I found it interesting that, while Arga seemed genuinely upset by the altercation, she appeared to view it as a sort of science experiment. She seemed interested to see what might happen next.

'Now I want you both to say sorry,' I said.

'*Nr!*' Arga bellowed.

'No,' Lonnie translated.

'I think I got that one, Lonnie,' I called back.

'What do you need me for?' my friend retorted. 'You're practically fluent.'

Tammy sat watching us.

'If you apologize, you'll both feel better. How can we have a party if everyone is trying to kill everyone else? That's no good.'

'*Uderzyła mnie!*' Arga seethed.

'She hit me,' Lonnie interjected. 'Or had you worked that one out too?'

'Tammy, did you hit Arga?' I asked, looking down at the tiny blond child.

She stared at her grimy, scuffed trainers, playing with one of the laces, twirling it about her finger.

137

'Did you, Tam?' I pressed. 'You know that's not a good thing to do.'

With lightning speed, Tammy let loose with a remarkably powerful punch to the bridge of my nose. It felt as if I had been kicked by a Shetland pony: tears sprang to my eyes and my hand flew to my face.

'Oh,' Arga said, pointing at Tammy, who sat right where she had been, watching my reaction with keen interest. '*Jesteś teraz w tarapatach! Jesteś zła, zła dziewczyna.*'

'She's giving out to her,' Lonnie said, wrestling with Mitzi, who was trying to eat a glove. 'Fill in the gaps yourself.'

I was hurt and annoyed. In my career in social care, I have been thumped, battered, kicked, burned and spat upon in just about every way imaginable. I do not resent it – it is very much a part of the job, and I am prepared to write it off against all the very powerful benefits the career offers. That said, I have never got used to being walloped in the face. I certainly don't like it, and I was in no doubt that, this time at least, I had not deserved it. I had not been rude to Tammy, my tone had been neutral and understanding – I had not even been cross with her.

I knew that if I stayed where I was, I would say something to the child I might later regret or, at the very least, have to apologize for, so I scooped Arga up in my arms and left Tammy where she was.

'Let's go and play with the doll's house,' I said, as we crossed the room.

'*Wszystko w porządku?*' Arga asked, stroking my cheek gently.

I had no idea what this meant, but I did as Lonnie had suggested, and filled in the gaps. 'I'm fine, honey. Yes, she did hurt me, but I'll survive.'

'*Ona jest zła dziewczyna.*'

'Maybe she's just having a bad day,' I said.

I sat Arga on a chair in front of the rather bruised doll's house we kept in a part of the room I was starting to think of as 'Lilliput' – there was a model of a town, some toy cars, a farm with plastic animals and the aforementioned house. Susan had told me that it was something of an antique, donated by a local woman whose children had grown up and moved away. She had said she wanted it to go to people who would love it as much as she had. Either the poor woman had not really liked it or she had made a mistake: the house looked as if it had been hit by a severe tornado, which was pretty close to what had happened since its arrival at Little Scamps.

Arga was looking at me with such concern on her little face that I had to laugh.

'Do you understand a word I'm saying to you?' I asked, brushing her hair back from her forehead.

She gazed back, frowning.

'Say . . . sorrrry . . .' she said.

I had no idea if these were the first English words she had ever spoken, but they were the first I had heard her say. I hugged her tight. 'I wonder if anyone ever said sorry to you. Because the world hasn't always been a nice place for you, has it?'

'Say sorrrry,' she said again, pressed into my chest.

'Yes,' I said. 'Thank you, Arga. Thank you.'

'Thanks . . . joo,' she said, looking at me with grave seriousness.

'Come on,' I said, turning her to look at the house. 'Let's have a game. What shall we play?'

'*Księżniczka!*' Arga said, clapping her hands.

I couldn't see any blank to fill in for that one, but Arga helped me by picking up a doll that was dressed like a princess, and began a commentary in Polish as the doll moved about the house. I watched her, trying to follow the story she was attempting to tell me. Out of the corner of my eye I spotted Tammy, standing a little away from us, watching closely. I was tempted to call her over, but was reminded by my smarting nose of why I had moved in the first place. I decided to ignore her, and see what happened.

Nothing happened.

Arga continued playing her game, occasionally handing me a doll and directing me through mime or gentle pushing in what she wished me to do with it. After twenty minutes or so it was time for outdoor play, and Arga, her scuffle forgotten, hugged me quickly and shot out of the door with the others. Tammy remained standing where she was.

'Time to go out now, Tam,' I said.

She gazed at me, unmoving.

'You mad at me?' I asked.

A curt nod.

'Well, if anyone has a reason to be angry, it's me. You hurt me quite badly.'

Tammy ran over and hugged my legs. My heart melted. I picked her up and gave her a cuddle.

'That's your way of telling me you didn't mean it, isn't it?' I asked her.

Another nod.

'Will we go outside now?'

She shook her head.

'So what do you want to do?'

She pointed at the books in the reading corner.

'You want a story?'

Nod.

'I'll tell you what, I'll read you a quick one and then we'll go outside to play. How's that?'

Tammy agreed, and we sat down among the beanbags again.

'What do you want to read?'

Tammy handed me one of my own favourites – *The Very Hungry Caterpillar* by Eric Carle. It's a wonderfully simple tale of a caterpillar that comes out of his egg one Sunday, spends the week eating his way through various different foods, after which he spins a cocoon and turns into a butterfly. The story is, of course, about growing up and the changes everyone goes through, but the illustrations are so beautifully rendered and such fun that children and adults alike disappear into it effortlessly.

I opened the first page, which featured a chunky, multi-coloured image of the eponymous caterpillar and the book's title. I was about to read it when a thought occurred to me.

'You know,' I said, Tammy snuggled up against my arm, 'in storybooks, the pictures often tell us what the words mean.'

Tammy's eyes were fixed on the picture. She jabbed the page with her finger as if to say, 'Come on, read it!'

'I'll bet you can't show me which word says "caterpillar",' I said.

Tammy looked up at me, an odd expression on her face – she was trying to read *me*. I just smiled innocently. Come on, Tammy, I thought. Show me what you can do! Without pausing, she pointed at the correct word. I felt my heart begin to beat a little faster. *She could read!* This child who, to all intents and purposes, appeared to be intellectually disabled might in fact be gifted. I reminded myself that picking out one word did not a competent reader make.

'That's absolutely right, Tammy,' I said gently. 'Well done. *The Very Hungry Caterpillar*. That's what this book is called, isn't it?'

She nodded, but I thought I detected suspicion in her

demeanour now. I turned the page and looked at the text. I didn't read it: 'In the light of the moon a little egg lay on a leaf.' The accompanying picture showed a richly hued night-time scene, with a delicate-looking, semi-transparent egg perched on a broad, curved leaf.

'Which word says "moon", Tammy?' I asked.

Her eyes on my face, a look of sullen rebellion on her own, Tammy put her finger on the word 'egg' and tapped it three times. I almost laughed. Something told me that if she really was unable to read, and the success of our first try had been a happy accident, she would have chosen a different word. The one that had the most letters in it, and therefore stood out (as 'caterpillar' had) was 'little'. 'Egg' had fewer letters, but was the other subject of the sentence. Tammy, I firmly believed, was playing with me. But I couldn't prove it, and she was telling me very clearly that she was not going to read for me any more, that day at least.

'Why don't I just finish the story and we can go outside?' I said.

And that was precisely what happened.

24

Susan had brought in a sort of graduated series of trays joined together with prettily coloured wire so we could display our cupcake creations for Milandra. There were also Krispie buns, some made with chocolate and some with marshmallow, and ice-cream (vanilla, strawberry and chocolate chip). The party was to happen in the hour before home-time.

'Jack them up on sugar and send them home to their parents – brilliant!' Lonnie had said, before bringing the kids outside with Tush so that Susan and I could get the place ready.

'I have a surprise of my own,' Susan said, when the food was set out.

'Yeah?' I said.

'I like your idea about the birthdays,' Susan said. 'I think we should make it a tradition – these things are important, and for some of our kids, a party here will probably be the only one they get. So, with that in mind . . .' She opened a cupboard over the craft table, and brought down a large box, wrapped in shiny pink paper.

'A present?' I said.

'I took the liberty of purchasing something I thought a

five-year-old girl might like,' Susan said. 'I had a notion you might find that a bit of a challenge.'

'Thanks, Susan,' I said, genuinely pleased. 'I appreciate your help on this. I know you've had some reservations about some of the changes I've made, but you've always tried to make things work.'

'We're all on the same side,' Susan said. 'But will you do me one favour in future?'

'Name it,' I said.

'Would you for fuck sake call me Su?'

The kids came back into the room in their usual manner: like a herd of stampeding cattle. They stopped dead in front of the cupcakes on their tiered tray. They did look spectacular – all the different colours and decorative touches Lonnie, Tush and I had used made them quite an impressive sight. With so many cupcakes – there were more than fifty – I thought that single birthday candles might get lost, so I had bought lots shaped as the number '5', and set those about the cakes. With the other treats and a few decorations we had hung about the room, Little Scamps had been transformed into Party Central.

'Wow!' Jeffrey said. 'Look at all de food!'

'Look at the candles,' Mitzi cooed. 'Bright and pretty. Like stars.'

Milandra was standing at the back of the crowd. So far that day she had been uncharacteristically quiet. There had been no angry outbursts, very little invective and no violence to either person or property. Milandra had kept herself to herself, and when we discussed the upcoming birthday celebrations at our breakfast meeting, she had not really got involved in the conversation, although we had been at pains to stress to her that this was *her* birthday, and the effort we had gone to was to honour and value her.

'What do you think, Milandra?' I asked, as she stood, mouth open, marvelling at the cakes.

'That whole pile of cakes is for me?' she asked, her voice barely audible.

'It is. Lonnie, Tush and I spent a long time on Saturday making them. I even made some special African ones, just like your dad would have eaten when he was a boy.'

Milandra laughed nervously. 'Yeah? African cakes like my daddy eats?'

'Come and see,' I said.

She walked up to the table.

I showed her the Colour Cakes. 'They taste of vanilla – 'cause Tush told me that's what you like – but as you can see, this one is green, and this one is pink, and this one is yellow. We put icing on them.'

Milandra seemed lost for words. She stood, holding my hand, trembling slightly. 'Them candles is number fives,' she said. 'That's my new age. I'm that age today, see, 'cause it's my birfday.'

'Yes, it is,' I said. 'And this is your party.'

Susan started singing 'Happy Birthday' and everyone joined in. Milandra laughed and clapped her hands. The party was off.

We played musical statues and pass-the-parcel (everyone won something), and then Milandra stood on a chair and blew out all her candles, a job that took three attempts.

'What did ya wish for, M'landra?' Rufus asked.

'You can't tell him 'cause then that wish won't come true,' Gus said. 'That's what my mammy always says.'

'No, it's okay,' Milandra said, one of her special Colour Cakes clutched in her hand, a candle still attached. 'I don' mind tellin'. I wished for a doll for my very own.'

145

'A doll?' Gus said. 'There's loads of dolls right here. Why'd you want an old doll?'

''Cause none o' them dolls looks like me,' Milandra said, and took a big bite of the cake.

Her comment hit me rather as Tammy's punch had. One of the basic lessons first-year childcare students are taught is to be acutely aware of anti-discriminatory practice, which means that all toys and images should be ethnically appropriate to all the children in your setting. Checking the room at a glance, and doing a mental run-through of the toys and storybooks we had, I realized that not a single one depicted any black children as central figures. I felt like slapping my head in annoyance – was there any wonder Milandra was so angry?

Making a mental note to rectify the omission as soon as possible, I went back to enjoying the party. To my delight, the cakes – even Lonnie's concoctions – were going down a treat. To my friend's credit, I tried his anchovy and caper cake, which he had iced with cream cheese and lemon, and it was actually very good.

With twenty minutes to go before the bus arrived, Susan called for quiet.

'Now, as it's Milandra's birthday, we thought it was only fair that she get a present,' Susan said. 'So, Milandra my dear, this is from everyone here at Little Scamps.'

Milandra looked as if she could not believe what was happening. Her blue eyes were wide, her mouth in a trembling smile. Susan took down the box, which elicited gasps and comments from everyone.

'That is one big present,' Ross said, clacking over on his crutches. 'D'ya need help openin' that, M'landra?'

'No. I can do it,' Milandra said, her voice high pitched with excitement, tearing at the paper with her nails.

The children had gathered around her in a loose circle, all eyes locked on the slowly emerging box. The wrapping finally came off in one huge swathe, and there, in a big red box with a clear plastic fronting, was Milandra's wish: a beautiful African doll with cornrowed hair, dressed in denim dungarees and shiny red shoes. I looked over at Susan and mouthed, *Well done!* She was grinning unashamedly.

Milandra opened the box and took the doll out, her eyes glistening, her lower lip trembling. 'For me?' she asked, turning to Susan, who had tears in her eyes, too.

'Yes, sweetie,' Susan said. 'Just for you. To show you that we all love you.'

'You all love me,' Milandra said, her voice breaking, the doll still clutched before her like some kind of talisman. 'This is my doll 'cause you all love me.'

I don't know what happened next. It was like somebody hit a switch and everything changed – changed utterly. One moment we were having one of those special, bitter-sweet moments that make childcare work worthwhile, the next all hell broke loose. Milandra's face turned into a scowl, she let loose a scream and ripped an arm off the doll with such force she tore the sleeve clean off its denim top. 'What the fuck is wrong with you all?' Milandra roared. 'Why'd you think I'd want a shitty doll like this? You all fucking hate me!'

Susan's mouth was working, but no words were coming out. I felt for her, but there was no time to offer comfort. Milandra was smashing the doll against the table repeatedly. Bang! Bang! Pop – the head flew off and hit Mitzi in the mouth, smearing the cupcake she had been eating right across her face.

'You shouldn't do that, treasure,' Mitzi said cheerily, and grabbed Milandra by the numerous ends of her cornrows.

The birthday girl was in such a fury she was operating on

pure instinct. Swinging the dismembered body of the doll, she caught Mitzi full in the throat and, amazingly, knocked her flat on her back. The other children were scattering, aware of the danger to life and limb. There was no way Milandra could be allowed to continue her rampage – someone had already been hurt. I came up behind her and wrapped my arms about her, pinning hers to her sides. She thrashed, trying desperately to kick me, but I sat down on the floor, tucked my chin away so it wouldn't get caught in a head-butt, and tried to relax. With my hands locked, one inside the other, it was impossible for her to get loose, so long as I didn't move. Which was not as easy as it sounds.

'Tush, can you stick with me, please?' I asked.

Tush was hovering nearby, uncertain what she should do. Lonnie had taken the rest of the kids outside, and Susan had gone too, although I didn't know how much good she'd be. Tush came over and sat cross-legged beside me.

'I need you to be able to record that I didn't hurt her or restrain her unnecessarily,' I explained. 'A kid should only be held like this as a last resort.'

Tush nodded. 'I know. I just got a bit . . . a bit flustered.'

'That's not a crime,' I said. 'Situations like this can be pretty unnerving. Just sit with me now and keep an eye on things. I need you to be my eyes from outside the restraint, all right?'

She nodded. During this entire conversation, Milandra continued to rage and roar, beating her head against my chest, snapping her teeth in an effort to bite any bit of me she could reach. I realized she still had the doll, what was left of it, clutched in her right hand in a death grip. She had gone beyond language now, her cries just strings of strangled noises: grunts, vocalizations and guttural squawks. Spittle dripped from her lips and ran in rivulets from the corner of her mouth.

'I can't see her eyes,' I said to Tush. 'Are they open? Can you see anything other than the whites?' I was concerned the child might be having a seizure brought on by the stress – a convulsion caused by a failure to breathe during the crisis, combined with the huge adrenaline rush she had experienced.

'I can see her pupils,' Tush said, coming as close as she dared. 'They're hugely dilated, though. I can barely see the iris.'

'Okay,' I said, sweat running down my forehead. 'She's conscious, at least.'

I could feel Milandra's rage like an electric hum. She was trembling, literally shaking with the force of her emotion. Usually a tantrum in a child so young will burn out within ten minutes or so. Fifteen had passed, and there was no sign that it was ending.

The other children filtered back in. I heard the bus pull up outside. Susan, her face still pale, ignored me and my noisy cargo. Lonnie came over and squatted next to my ear. 'You okay there, *amigo*?'

'I'm holding up,' I said.

'She's one tough little cookie,' Lonnie observed. 'How much longer d'you think she can keep it up?'

'I have no idea,' I said. 'How much longer can *I*?'

Lonnie laughed and patted me on the shoulder.

'Oh, you're only getting warmed up.'

'There's no way we can put her on the bus,' I said. 'She'd cause a crash.'

'So what's the alternative?'

'I hold her until she calms down, then Tush and I will bring her home. You all right with that, Tush?'

'Sure,' Tush said.

Lonnie nodded. 'All righty, then. Do I take it that I have custody of Millie tonight?'

I grinned through the strain. 'I think that might be wise,' I said. 'Better to be safe than sorry.'

Lonnie stood. 'Maybe I should have my lawyer draw up some sort of agreement,' he said. 'I think you're taking advantage of my good nature. You just assume I'll take her any time you feel like swanning off. It's not good enough.'

'You're such a prima donna,' I said.

'I'll remember you said that, you bitch,' Lonnie said. 'See you later.'

It took Milandra an hour to run out of steam. Her bellows fell off into dull moans, and then to a sort of intermittent whimpering. From where I sat I could see the child's struggles mirrored in Tush's face – the poor girl seemed to feel every wave of pain Milandra experienced. I admired her for it. Such profound empathy is rare, even among childcare workers.

When Milandra had been silent for five minutes, I felt her sag against me and knew exhaustion had finally taken her. 'Honey, I'm going to let go,' I said. 'But first I want you to promise that you're not going to attack either me or Tush, and that you're not going to run away, or try to smash the room up. Do we have a deal?'

There was no response.

'I know you're tired, sweetie, but you're going to have to answer me, or I'm going to keep holding on to you. I don't want to, but I won't have a choice.'

'I'll be good,' Milandra whimpered. 'I won't try 'n' hurt nobody. I promise.'

I released my arms, and the little girl slid on to the floor and stayed there. I staggered up and nearly fell over: my legs had gone to sleep. Using the wall I made it to a chair and sat there, massaging the blood back into circulation. Tush went over to Milandra and stroked her head, talking gently to her. 'You feel better, baby girl?' she asked.

'I feel sick,' Milandra said.

'You think you're going to be sick?'

'Yeah!'

Milandra rolled over and threw up a brightly complexioned mixture of semi-digested Colour Cake and juice on to the floor. She continued to retch for a few minutes, then seemed to be a little better, so Tush brought her down to the bean bags and made her comfortable, putting a blanket over her.

'She's worn herself out,' Tush said, as we cleaned up the vomit.

'Her and us too,' I said.

'What the hell set her off?' Tush asked. 'I mean, I've never seen her happier. It was one of the nicest moments we've had since I've been here. Then – I don't know what happened. It was like she turned into a different child, like something else took over.'

'I don't know,' I said. We went into the kitchen and emptied the bucket of disinfectant-laced water. 'I've worked with kids before who didn't believe they deserved to be happy. They railed against it, caused things to go wrong in their lives every time situations looked like improving. I wonder if that's what Milandra does. Today it was as if the idea that she was loved was just too much for her to cope with.'

Tush wrung out the mop. 'But why? Isn't being loved a good thing?'

I thought about that. 'Want some coffee?'

'Please.'

I put on the kettle and spooned some grounds into the cafetière. 'When people love you, particularly if you love them back, they can hurt you – you make yourself vulnerable.

151

If you think everybody hates you, well, it's no big deal when they let you down. For a kid who really fears rejection, being hated might be a lot easier.'

Tush looked glumly at the kettle as it started to steam. 'She's so young to be thinking in that way.'

'I don't reckon any of it's conscious. But I think that is one very confused and unhappy little girl.'

Tush sighed deeply. 'So what do we do about it?'

'Well,' I said, 'when she wakes up, we take her home and have a very long and frank discussion with her parents.'

'Oh, good,' Tush said. 'I love confrontation.'

When the coffee was made I rang Milandra's home, and spoke to her grandmother, explaining as briefly as I could what had happened and that we would be dropping the child home as soon as she was fit to travel.

It was another two hours before we were all in Tush's Volkswagen Golf. Milandra had woken up and asked for a drink of water, then meekly said she would like to go home, please. She sat in the back seat, gazing out of the window, treating Tush and me as if we were not there.

Tush knew the way to Milandra's – which was just as well, because I had only a vague recollection, and was too tired to think deeply about it. We were there within forty minutes. The child looked so drained when we parked outside the detached bungalow, one of ten on a tree-lined street, that I asked her if she'd like me to carry her. To my great surprise, she nodded. I scooped her up in my arms and took her to the front door.

Our ring was answered by a very beautiful blond woman dressed in a crisp white shirt and designer jeans. I would have put her at around my own age – thirty-five years old. She had concern writ large across her sculpted face. 'I'm Felicity,

Landra's mother,' she said, holding out her arms for the little girl. 'Please come in.'

We followed her into a tastefully decorated hallway and through to the living room.

'She's had quite an afternoon, I'm afraid,' I said. 'Gave us something of a scare.'

Milandra wrapped her arms around her mother's neck, her head resting on her shoulder.

'I'm so sorry,' Felicity said. 'She's always been very highly strung.'

'My concern is that she could have hurt Mitzi badly,' I said. 'Does she fly into these blind rages at home?'

'Almost every day,' Felicity said, laughing nervously. 'Sometimes she scares me, too. I don't know what gets into her.'

'She's a very clever girl,' Tush said. 'She can read well above the standard for her age, and her levels of numeracy are excellent. She should be at school. It's her behaviour that's stopping her.'

'What should I do?' Felicity said. 'My mother says we over-indulge her. That we should spank her.'

'I'm not suggesting that for a second,' I said, 'but maybe you do need to set some clear boundaries and stick with them. Milandra must see that violence and aggression are unacceptable ways of expressing herself.'

As I said this, a door opened behind me and a tall, extremely handsome man came out, wearing what looked to be an expensive suit, his top button open and his silk tie hanging loose.

'Tony, these are the workers from Landra's crèche,' Felicity said.

The man walked straight up to me and came very close. We would have been nose to nose had I been taller, but I found myself peering at his ample chest. I had to raise my head to look him in the eye.

'You have trouble handling my daughter, Mr Dunphy?'

'No,' I said, hardly believing what I was hearing. 'I think I handled her quite well actually.'

'I heard she broke things, attacked other children,' Tony continued. He pronounced every word very precisely. 'You cannot keep your charges under control.'

'I don't think it's appropriate for two of the adults in your daughter's life to be having a conversation like this while she's upset,' I said.

'Because I'm coming close to the truth,' Tony said. 'This makes you uncomfortable.'

'You're making me feel uncomfortable, all right,' I said. 'Come on, Tush.'

'Your job is not an honourable one for a man to do,' Tony said, as I walked towards the door. 'In my country, only one kind of man works with children.'

I spun around, trying to keep anger in check. I had heard this opinion countless times in my career, but I was tired, sore – and utterly pissed off by this man's antagonistic attitude.

'Tell me,' I said, 'what kind of man works with children in your country.'

'We call him *ôkùnrin ábökùnrinlò*,' Tony said, smiling like a crocodile might smile at a tapir that has wandered too close to the wrong watering-hole.

'Tony, stop right now,' Felicity said. 'These people are our guests.'

'That's quite all right,' I said. 'And what does that mean?'

'I'm sure you are a resourceful man,' my host said. 'Why don't you find out?'

Tush took my arm. 'Come on, Shane. I think we should go.'

'Yes, your lady would like to leave, now,' Tony said.

He took Milandra from Felicity's arms and kissed her. 'You have been a naughty girl, have you, precious?'

Milandra nodded and cuddled into her father.

'You are a fierce warrior, are you not?' he said.

Sickened, I let Tush lead me out.

Tush said nothing when we got into the car, but she drove like a woman possessed down the narrow country roads, not slowing down until we were two villages away.

'That fucking horrible, *horrible* man!' she said, tears starting to stream down her cheeks as she finally let the frustration and unfairness of the experience come to the fore.

'He's a keeper all right,' I said.

She looked at me in disbelief, then burst out laughing. 'I thought he was going to kill you,' she said.

'He's a bit scary,' I agreed. 'Easy to see where Milandra gets it from.'

'What did he call you?'

'I can't remember, to be honest, but I know what it means.'

'Oh?'

'It'd be Yoruba for "eunuch" or "homosexual" or "ladyboy" or something of that nature.'

'Because you work with kids.'

'Yup. I've heard it a million times before, and in several languages, actually.'

'Do you know what's kind of a pity?' Tush asked.

'What?'

'That Lonnie wasn't there. I'd have loved to see what Tony and Lonnie would have made of one another.'

It was my turn to laugh. Indeed, Lonnie's reaction to Tony's absurd machismo would have been priceless.

'You like him a lot, don't you?' I asked Tush.

'He's great, yeah.'

'Don't you start acting tough on me!' I said. 'It's not a bad thing to have feelings for someone.'

She glanced at me from the corner of her eye, tapping the steering wheel with her fingers as if it were a bongo drum. 'Yeah. I do like him. He's one of the most amazing people I've ever met. He's funny and cute and brainy, and he's great with the kids.'

'So,' I said, 'are you going to tell him?'

'I don't know how,' she said. 'He's a bit older than me and he has so much experience, and I just feel so . . . so young and stupid when I'm around him.'

'Jesus, you're a right fucking pair,' I said.

I could have told her that she was, in all likelihood, twice as worldly wise as Lonnie, that their age was irrelevant and that he was just as mad about her as she was about him, but I kept my mouth shut. Nature would, I hoped, take its course. In the meantime, all I wanted was a glass of whiskey, something to eat and a good night's sleep. The rest of the world's problems would just have to wait.

25

I woke up the next day feeling as if I hadn't slept a wink, although I had actually turned in for the night at just before nine. I made some scrambled eggs and poured a glass of juice and took it out to the garden. It was already shaping up to be a lovely day, and the birdsong was a welcome alternative to the bad news that dominated on the radio.

I wanted to spend time doing something light and pleasant. The wretchedness of the previous day had left me with no appetite for difficulty or drama. What could we do in Little Scamps that would help take our minds off the troubles that so often hung over the little group like storm clouds? I watched a mistle thrush, perched on one of my gate posts, singing its heart out, and the answer came to me.

'"Whistle while you work,"' I said to the bird, toasting it with my glass. 'Hum a merry tune.'

'Is that a toy?' Gilbert asked.

He was looking at my ukulele, which, for the uninitiated, looks like a tiny toy guitar with four strings. If you study the history of the instrument you will find that Gilbert was far from the first person to question if such a frivolous-seeming item could be a legitimate part of the musical pantheon – back in the 1920s the Musicians Union of America had debated whether or not uke players should be permitted membership. A formidable lady called May Breen persuaded it that they certainly should, and in one fell swoop cemented the instrument's place in folk and jazz history.

I had decided that the ukulele was the ideal accompaniment for a music session: it has a light, deft tone, and seems somehow less serious than other instruments – it's difficult to play a mournful song on a uke.

'No,' I told Gilbert and everyone else. 'This is not a toy. Listen.'

I played a D-seventh chord in tremolo, and the group clapped loudly. Milandra had not come in, which, sad to say, had lightened the general mood: everyone was a little relieved.

'Now, I know you're all really good singers because I've heard you sing lots of times,' I said. 'Today I want to teach you a new song. It's very easy to learn, and it's all about animals.'

'Like bunny rabbits?' Rufus asked.

'Well, I'm not sure there are any rabbits in *this* song,' I said, 'but there are lots of other animals of all kinds.'

'Moo cows?' Jeffrey said.

'I'll tell you what,' I said. 'I'm going to sing it. I want you to join in and help me out because, d'you know, I might not be able to remember all the words. It's been a very long time since I sang this one. Will you give me a hand?'

The children said they would help, as did Susan (still pale and refusing to talk about Birthdaygate), Tush and Lonnie.

I played a short introduction, a simple finger pick between the G and D-seventh chords, then began to sing.

The first verse is all about how wonderful elephants are, and illustrates this point by commenting on how they love to eat bananas and swing from tree to tree. Of course, by the time I was halfway through the line, half the children in the group had shouted me down. I pretended to be surprised at the interruption. 'What? What's wrong?'

'That's not elephants!' Rufus said. 'That's a monkey.'

'Oh,' I said, scratching my head. 'Are you sure?'

'Yeah,' Ross said. 'Dat should def'n'y be monkeys dere.'

'Okay, then,' I said. 'Here we go again.'

I began the next verse by singing about how I liked monkeys, particularly how they loved to swim in the ocean. I barely got the first word of that line out.

'No! That's fish you're thinkin' of,' Gus said.

'Fish?' I said. 'Well, I told you I hadn't sung this song for a long time.'

The fish in the next verse scratched at fleas and barked at the postman. The kids were laughing now. They'd realized it was a game, and jumped right in before I had a chance to move on.

'Tha's a dog!' Jeffrey said.

We had dogs who curled up on the windowsill, purred and chased mice, cats who said 'cock-a-doodle-doo', roosters that lived in the forest and stole honey from beehives, bears that sat on lilypads and ate flies, frogs that lived in holes in the wall and ate cheese . . . We had great fun with the song (written by a hugely talented children's entertainer called Eric Herman), and when we finally got to the end (it's easy to string it out to nearly ten minutes) the children called for it again. I got a great kick out of watching them waiting for me to make the mistakes. I made different ones this time, mixing it up so they would have to identify each creature as I attributed its characteristics to a totally different hairy, feathered or scaled beast.

When I had completed my encore, I invited the children

to sing something for me. They were not backward about coming forward. Jeffrey sang a rather unusual version (in that it had no discernible melody) of 'Molly Malone' and we all joined in with gusto. Ross sang the chorus of 'The Fields of Athenry' about ten times (Lonnie finally stopped him by clapping loudly). Arga sang something in Polish, which Lonnie explained was an old folk song.

But it was Mitzi who surprised us all. When Arga had finished her song Mitzi slid off her chair so she was actually standing (a rare occurrence in itself) and began to sing in a soft, unbelievably sweet voice. It was a song from that bastion of 1970s television, *The Muppet Show*, called *The Rainbow Connection*, usually performed by Kermit the Frog, accompanying himself on a five-string banjo. The song is about hope, loss and belief in the inherent decency of people. I wondered where she could have heard it, and assumed her parents must have taught her – they were hippie types, after all, and the beautiful mysticism of the lyric has been adopted by all sorts of groups and wrapped around many different interpretations since it first became popular thirty-odd years ago.

When Mitzi finished her rendition she gave an awkward, shy curtsy and tried to get back on to her chair – unsuccessfully. Tush had to go over and help.

'That was amazing, Mitzi,' Lonnie said, when the applause died down.

'I never heard you singin' afore, Mitzi,' Ross said. 'How come?'

'A girl likes to have her secrets, children,' Mitzi said, twiddling her thumbs and smiling to herself.

'Well, I, for one, would like to hear more from you,' I said. 'You're a very talented lady.'

'I have the voice of an angel, yes, I do,' Mitzi agreed.

'I'll be calling on you again, angel,' I said. 'So you'd better do some practising.'

At lunch I sat outside with Susan.

'How you doing?' I asked.

'Not so good,' she admitted. 'I can't believe I misread Milandra so badly. I thought I knew her. She's been with us since she was three years old. How could I have been so wrong?'

'I don't think you were.'

'How do you make that out?'

'You heard her wish – you gave her exactly what she wanted. It was like you'd read her mind, for Chrissakes. But you've heard the saying "Be careful what you wish for." I think she got what she wanted, and it scared the bejesus out of her.'

Susan was sitting on the wooden rim of the sand container, a mug of tea cupped between her hands. 'Explain.'

'I worked with a kid in residential care once, a long time ago. He was my key-child – I had special responsibility for him – and I thought he was a great young fella, a real sweetheart. But life had dealt him a rough hand. He'd been orphaned when he was a baby, and shoved around from pillar to post between a lot of different care settings. So he was angry a lot of the time. Not like Milandra – he didn't smash things or hit people. He was just . . . sad, I suppose.'

'Poor kid.'

'Yeah. My first Christmas with him he told me the one thing he wanted was a bike. And not just any bike. He had gone down to the local bicycle shop and picked out a beautiful red Chopper.'

'Is that a cool bike?'

'Yeah. Pretty damn cool.'

'So you got it for him?'

'Ah, if only it were that simple. You see, for my little boy, this bike became so much more than just a Christmas present. He talked about it day and night. "When I get my bike on Christmas morning, I'm going to do this or that." Like "When I have my bike, I'll be the fastest kid on the street. When my bike comes, everyone is going to want a ride on it." This bicycle was going to be the best thing ever to happen in his life.'

'The cure for all his ills.'

'Exactly. Except there was a problem. I had a budget to purchase gifts for him, and I can tell you, this bike was way, way beyond that amount. I went to my boss and I begged and pleaded, but he *couldn't* budge. So I went over his head, to the care manager. He agreed, after no small amount of weeping and wailing on my behalf, to stump up the extra few quid. And I got the bike.'

'Was your boy happy?'

I laughed sadly. 'For about an hour. Now remember, he wasn't like Milandra – he didn't throw it off a bridge or set fire to it. He started to find fault. Why didn't I tell him the bell sounded like that? Why weren't the handlebars wider? Surely it was a brighter red in the shop – had I even got the right one? By five o'clock Christmas night, he was up in his room crying his eyes out, shouting that I had ruined Christmas.'

'And in a way you had,' Susan said.

'That's right. By giving him exactly what he wanted.'

'Because it *wasn't* what he wanted at all.'

I put my own cup down and yawned in the sunlight. I was tired, but happy with how the day had gone so far. 'No, it wasn't what he wanted. He wanted his parents back, and not to be in care any more, and never to wake up with that hole full of sadness inside him. Somehow, in his confusion and pain, he got to believing a new red Chopper would give him all those things.'

'But it didn't,' Susan said.

'No. It was just a bike. A cool bike, but just a bike for all that.'

Susan nodded and looked wistfully at our ragamuffin bunch of children, playing a game of tag among the play equipment, with Lonnie as It.

'So what does Milandra really want, then? She has two parents who seem to love her, a nice house, she's pretty and smart . . . I don't get it.'

I shrugged. 'Damned if I know. From what I could see, her dad seems to encourage her aggression.'

'Yeah, I heard he was a bit of a prick, all right,' Susan said.

'We're just going to have to watch this space, and see what emerges,' I said. 'But, more pressingly, what did you make of Mitzi?'

We both looked over at her, sitting in a corner of the yard on her own, eating a peanut-butter sandwich.

'She's a dark horse, isn't she?' Susan said.

'She is,' I said, 'but she let her guard down.'

'How?'

'The kid has a lot of raw talent,' I said, 'but she must have practised some, too. She loves to sing. Other than eating and being a bit evil, have we ever known anything else Mitzi likes to do?'

Susan grinned. 'No, we haven't.'

'The question,' I said slowly, 'is how we can use this new information to make Mitzi a happier, healthier little girl.'

It was a problem that had both of us stumped.

26

Days blurred into weeks and weeks into months. Little Scamps punctuated the rhythm of my life, and without even realizing it, I fell in love with the place and the children who made it such an infuriating, heart-warming and challenging place to work. No two days were the same: every time I walked through the front door I knew without doubt that something would test me to the extreme, and welcomed it. I was learning in ways I never had before, and it was an exciting, gratifying experience.

Productivity in childcare cannot be measured in the same way as it is in other professions – the developmental steps small children take are often so tiny that even the people who work in the area can miss them. Yet I *could* see improvement. Progress was obvious to me, and my colleagues told me they could see it too. The violence, chaos and mayhem that had once characterized each day still erupted from time to time, but now it was a rarity rather than the norm.

Tammy remained implacable, although there were some chinks of light through the darkness she seemed to carry about with her. Sonya Kitchell at Tiny Flowers had proven that punishment was not going to induce her to be more expressive, so I began to wonder what we might use as a reward – I hoped to reinforce the behaviour we wanted to encourage.

I watched Tammy closely when she ate to see if I could work out what her favourite treats were. This proved to be utterly fruitless – she hoovered up everything we put in front of her without any comment, good, bad or indifferent. I tried varying the contents of her lunchbox hoping to judge by positive reactions, to no avail. I set out different items at breakfast, but that, too, was a waste of time. Finally, I determined that Tammy, like most other kids, would probably, given the choice, favour sweet things. I baked a batch of the oatmeal and raisin biscuits she had previously eaten without complaint, and kept a couple in my pocket, ready to reward any particularly communicative acts.

I wondered if she somehow picked up a subtle change in my demeanour, because days passed without her making so much as eye-contact with me. When eventually she shook her head and grunted at me, a full week had gone by and I didn't have a biscuit within reach. Cursing myself, I made a fresh batch and determined to be more patient. This time I was rewarded.

'That's a great picture, Tammy,' I said. 'Want to tell me about it?'

Tammy shook her head firmly.

I grinned. 'That's okay,' I said. 'I'm just glad you answered me. Would you like a biscuit?'

Tammy looked puzzled, but held out her hand for the treat.

'I'd love you to talk, Tam,' I said, 'but only when you're ready. And in the meantime, maybe you could let me know how you feel about things by nodding a bit more, or doing *anything* to help me know what's going on in your head.'

Tammy crunched up the biscuit, her eyes fixed on me. When it was gone she slid down from her chair and walked away, leaving me sitting where I was. She did not so much as grunt in my direction for two weeks after that.

It looked as if bribery wasn't going to work.

Autumn came in with the smell of turf fires and home-baked bread. The narrow roads about our village were scattered with the spiky shells of horse chestnuts, the fields covered with drifts of crisp brown leaves. The roadside hedges and trees sagged under the weight of berries and fruit. One morning Rufus's mother, who was spending the day with us, made a suggestion: 'We should make jam.'

'I'm not sure about the children working with molten sugar, Bridie,' I said to her.

It had taken six weeks for her to decide to share her first name with us, but she had thawed rapidly after that. I had also seen a notable improvement in her relationship with her son. Rufus was cleaner, better fed and generally happier.

'Sure they don't have to *make* the jam. They can help pick the fruit, weigh it out and that. It'd be fun.'

The following day, the entire complement from Little Scamps was trekking across the fields, buckets in hand, searching for blackberries and crab apples.

'I'm just like Peter Rabbit,' Ross said.

'Well, you're more like Peter Rabbit's sisters,' I said. 'Peter decided not to go blackberry picking, and stole from Mr McGregor instead.'

'No, I'm definitely like Peter Rabbit,' Ross insisted.

'How?' I said.

'I've just stoled a load of berries from Jeffrey's bucket.' Ross cackled, scooting away from Jeffrey's punch.

I had tried to erase Peter Rabbit from their memories but the naughty creature had proved to be remarkably tenacious. They mentioned him often, comparing a vast array of experiences to his exploits, and seeming to find endless uses for the moral lessons the story posed. Its profound impact had presented me with an opportunity I should not pass up. I planned to return to Beatrix Potter. I was just waiting for the right time.

'Now, ye have to look close to the ground for the blackberries,' Bridie told the children, pulling aside a leafy branch and showing them a bramble bush heavy with juicy black fruit. 'But the crab apples, which will make the jam *extra* tasty, they live higher up. See there?'

Using a stick she pointed out the small red apples that hung in bunches above the heads of the children. Like a shot, Rufus scaled the tree she indicated and tossed the apples down to his mother, who caught them in her bucket.

This almost caused me to have a coronary – and it encouraged the other climber in the group. Tammy took it upon herself to see if she could beat Rufus to the hard little fruits, and soon the pair were racing up the narrow, spindly trees.

'Come on now, one of you is going to fall!' I said, as Rufus tried to kick Tammy back to the ground.

'Ah, sure it'll do them no harm.' Bridie laughed. 'If they fall once or twice, it makes them all the more careful next time.'

'If they end up in the hospital, *I* won't get a chance to be more careful next time,' I said. 'I'll be unemployed.'

Bridie tutted. 'Tell me this, Mr Safety Man. Do you think Tammy's mammy or daddy will cause any fuss if she comes home with a bruise on her arm or a bump on her head?'

I watched the climbers reach some sort of agreement as they took turns in tossing down the apples. 'I don't suppose they will,' I said.

'Then why don't you relax and let them have some fun? What's healthier than children climbin' a tree for apples?'

I had to agree with her.

And it was probably the nicest jam I've ever tasted.

27

All the lights in the crèche were switched off, and the curtains drawn to block out the dwindling sunlight. The only illumination came from several frighteningly carved Hallowe'en pumpkins. (In fact, they looked more friendly than frightening – Tush had been in charge of giving them faces and they looked to me as if they were smiling.) Lonnie had found a CD of scary noises – chains rattling, evil laughter, werewolves howling, thunder booming and the like, but it had scared Julie, so we had abandoned it in favour of a *Bear in the Big Blue House* collection, which was not at all seasonal but unlikely to give anyone nightmares.

We had played all sorts of games, and would soon have some stories, but now the children were about to embark on the game they had been looking forward to all day: the Lucky Dip. Susan had come up with the idea, and it was very simple: every child had to answer a question (tailor made so they would have no difficulty with it) that gave them access to the huge box filled with shredded paper and the prizes. Turns were chosen by lottery: Lonnie pulled names out of a hat.

'Okay, I've got Gus,' he said. 'Are you ready for your question, Gus, my man?'

'Yes, I am,' Gus said, more than a little nervous.

'All right, here we go. What colour – and I need the exact colour, mind – is Tush's car?'

Gus paused for a moment, his face scrunched up in concentration. 'Blue!' he said jubilantly.

'Go and get your prize!' Lonnie said.

Gus spent ages rooting around in the box, and came out with a parcel covered with pictures of witches and bats. He ripped off the paper – it was a colouring book and crayons. Gus whooped and danced about as if he had just found a cheque for a million euro.

So it went on – everyone got a prize and, thankfully, everyone seemed more than happy with their acquisition. We all took a deep breath when Milandra had her go, but she liked the set of Hallowe'en stickers she received – and even gave Lonnie a hug.

When everyone was done, we sat in a circle, the music turned down, only one pumpkin left lighting the room.

'Do you all remember *Peter Rabbit*?' I asked.

Nods and yeses all around.

'Do you remember I told you that story was written by a lady named Beatrix Potter?'

Less agreement this time – most of the children had probably forgotten that detail.

'Well, Beatrix wrote lots of children's stories, and I'd like to read you another one today. It's scary, in a nice kind of way, and it's about an animal a lot of people associate with Hallowe'en: the rat!'

The kids made faces and noises of disgust, but they were having fun already.

The story I read was *The Tale of Samuel Whiskers*. It had always scared me a little as a kid – Beatrix Potter had again indulged her dark sensibilities, but I thought it just frightening enough to give our gang a thrill, but not so terrifying any of them would get upset.

As in *Peter Rabbit*, the story revolves around a naughty child. Tom Kitten lives with his mother, Mrs Tabitha Twitchit, and sisters, Moppet and Mittens, in a house overrun with rats. Her children being an unruly bunch, Mrs Twitchit puts Moppet and Mittens in a cupboard in order to keep them under control – the equivalent of sending them to their room – but Tom Kitten escapes up the chimney. As he makes his way to the top of the house, he comes across a crack in the wall and, squeezing through it, finds himself under the attic's floorboards.

I liked this element of the story particularly – every child fantasizes about a portal to another world. C. S. Lewis had based his Narnia books on the idea, as had Enid Blyton with her *Faraway Tree* stories, and J. K. Rowling in the Harry Potter books. The crux of these literary journeys is: if you manage to make the passage from your own world to another, will you be able to get back – and will you want to? *The Tale of Samuel Whiskers* is no different.

When Tom Kitten finds himself in the world beneath the floor, he meets the rats, Mr Samuel Whiskers and his wife Anna Maria. They catch him, then cover him with butter and dough to turn him into a pudding and eat him. However, when they start to roll out the dough, the noise attracts the attention of Tabitha Twitchit and her friend Ribby, who have been searching for Tom. They quickly call for John Joiner, the carpenter, who saws open the floor and rescues Tom.

Samuel Whiskers and his wife escape to the barn of Farmer Potatoes. Potter adds as a sort of postscript that she saw Samuel Whiskers and Anna Maria making their escape, using a wheelbarrow that looked very like her own.

I had again got the pictures enlarged, and we discussed

each one. The children had tremendous fun and I could tell that they had identified easily with Tom Kitten: his awful situation involved creatures with which they were all familiar. One cannot live in the country for long without coming in contact with rats, and the children were well aware that their parents hated them.

'How did Tom find himself in so much trouble?' I asked.

'Climb up de chimbley,' Jeffrey said.

'That's right,' I said. 'Now, you couldn't do that in the houses we live in today, because you just wouldn't fit, but when Beatrix Potter was writing, the houses had great big chimneys, and they would often send children right up inside to clean them. Can you imagine that?'

There was much debate.

'You remember Tom's mum put his sisters in the cupboard because they were so naughty and she needed a break?' I said. 'Have you ever been asked to stay in your room, but then you didn't?'

Almost every head in the circle nodded.

'One time, I sneakeded out of my room,' Milandra said.

'Did you?' I asked.

'Yeah.' She nodded. 'Mammy and Daddy was havin' a dinner party wit their friends. I could hear them talkin' and I sneakeded downstairs. I went into the kitchen and I tooked some stuff out of the fridg'rator.'

'What kinda stuff, M'landra?' Ross asked.

'Stuff in a bottle. It was a big green bottle, wit a twisty top. I drinked it, and I gotted sick. It was *scustin*'!'

'Mmm,' I said. 'I think that might have been stuff only grown-ups are meant to drink, sweetie.'

'My dad whipped me good,' she said.

I frowned. Milandra's mother had told me they didn't slap the child. 'Did he?' I asked.

171

'He said I could've pysened myself,' she said gravely.

'Well, that's true,' I said, and changed the subject.

It was puzzling, though.

Lonnie approached me as we were cleaning up. 'Great story,' he said.

'Thanks.'

I could tell he had something on his mind, but I knew he'd get to it in his own time. It didn't take long.

'I've let it slide, but I can't keep my mouth shut any more,' he blurted.

'What's that?' I asked patiently.

'D'you remember, when I started at Little Scamps, what the main project – which was going to save the whole bloody crèche – was? Remember how this room was empty, most of the furniture was outside or in the kitchen? Remember all that?'

I knew where he was going, but thought it might be fun to see how we'd get there. 'Of course the place was like that. We were redecorating.'

Lonnie laughed cacophonously. 'Every single item of furniture is back inside, all the toys are in, and we've done countless projects and activities to help us think up pictures to *put* on the goddam wall . . .'

'Yeah?' I said, feeding his temper.

'But not one single bloody picture has been painted on it!'

Indeed the walls were still white from floor to ceiling, although we *had* now stuck some posters on them in some places. The tins of paint were stacked at the back of the room, near the door to the outdoor play area, and Tush had put a tarpaulin over them. Not so much as one bristle from a paintbrush had been dipped into them since that first day.

'And your point is?' I said to my irate friend.

'You're a total spoofer!' he said in disgust.

'I'm surprised it took you so long to notice,' I said, slapping him on the back as I walked past.

28

It is a constant source of amazement to me that monumental events can so often appear utterly insignificant. If only we could see the signs when they present themselves, grasp the meaning that is buried within mundane happenings before it is obscured by time and conflicting factors.

The children were lining up for their bus. The room was almost back to normal and I was pushing chairs and tables into their original places. The only person who was refusing to co-operate was Gus. He was bent over his new colouring book, a thick blue crayon from his pack clutched in his hand, hard at work.

'Time to wrap it up for today, Augustus,' I said.

'This was a really good prize to win in the Lucky Dip,' Gus said, still busy.

'I'm thrilled you like it so much,' I said. 'But you can do more when you get home, can't you?' I sat down next to him. 'Whatcha doing anyway?'

'Colourin',' he said, answering my painfully stupid question with great patience.

'I can see that,' I admitted.

'Want me to tell ya sumpin?'

'I sure do.'

'This crayon – this *blue* crayon, which is my favouritest colour – is magic.'

I considered this profound statement.

'Is that so?'

'Yes. With this crayon, see, I can colour inside the lines and I *never ever ever* go outside – lessen I wants to.'

He was colouring a picture of a boat on a wavy ocean, with seagulls in the sky and a dolphin with a smiley face poking out of the water, seeming to wave at the sailors. Gus had coloured bits and pieces of the image in blue, and, sure enough, he had kept perfectly within the lines.

'That's really cool,' I said. 'A magic crayon is a fine thing for a boy to have.'

'Mmm-hmm,' Gus said, still focused on the task at hand.

'But it's time for you to get your coat and all your gear, and head for the bus!' I said, ruffling his hair.

'Okay.' He sighed.

Several months later I realized what had happened that evening and the magic became real.

Things had stalled somewhat with Tammy, and I was starting, if not to panic, then to become seriously worried. We would sit together as a group and I would watch the other children laughing and jabbering away nineteen to the dozen, but the little blond enigma would sit there as if she were encased in a hermetically sealed capsule, utterly unmoved by anything that was going on. In the dark hours of the night I would often pore over her case in my head, convinced that I had missed something, overlooked a detail, a clue that would unlock the chains that bound her so deeply inside herself.

I came up with nothing.

Desperation drove me to direct my efforts to the most

obvious place – her family. Not wanting to risk encountering a drunken Dale or Kylie, I decided to visit on a Saturday morning. At ten thirty I pulled up outside the little house, the cry of gulls plaintive on the wind, salt lingering on the air. The road was deserted as I knocked on the door, and I wondered if Kylie and Dale were the only people who lived in these houses – in the few times I had been there, I had never seen anyone else. My knocks elicited no response, so I banged louder. This time I saw a curtain twitch, and Tammy's little face pressed up against the glass on the other side. I waved. She looked back at me blankly. I could almost hear her brain working: *What's going on? He's not meant to be here today!* She did not move, so I hammered on the door again. This time I could hear dull thudding inside the building, and at last the door was opened by a very ill-looking Kylie.

'What?' she snapped.

'Hi, Kylie,' I said. 'Remember me? Shane, from Little Scamps?'

She shook her head, then stopped abruptly and placed a hand on her temple as if to still the pain. I was under no illusion as to the reason she might not be feeling the best – she reeked of booze.

'What the fuck do you want so early on a Saturday morning?' she hissed.

'To have a chat with you about Tammy,' I said gently. 'Will I make us some coffee? You look like you could use some.'

'I don't feel well,' Kylie said. 'In fact, I think I'm going to be sick. Please leave me alone.' She began to close the door.

'Can I come back later?'

She never answered. The door slammed shut. I stood there. Tammy was still gazing at me through the window, as if she was frozen there. I waved half-heartedly and walked back to the car. I sat inside and looked at the rolling scrub of the salt marsh. I checked the clock on the dashboard. The entire altercation had taken all of three minutes. I switched on the engine – I wasn't done yet. I would give Kylie some time to recover, and then I'd come back. I was nothing if not persistent.

One thirty. I had killed a few hours reading the morning paper, drinking coffee and walking on the beach. Now I was feeling bright, full of sea air and ready for another tilt at Kylie. I knocked.

When she answered she looked a little less green about the gills, but was still wearing her night clothes and smelling strongly of alcohol. 'What the fuck do you want?' she barked.

'Can I come in?' I asked. 'I won't take up much of your time – I just want to talk to you about Tammy.'

'What do you want to tell me about Tammy that I don't know?'

'I—'

'Or have you come to lecture me about not lookin' after her right?'

'No, I—'

'Maybe you want me to come and help out in that fuckin' crèche. I heard some of the tinkers are doin' that.'

'Well—'

'Just fuck off right back to where you came from,' Kylie said. 'Do your job, mind Tammy durin' the week, and leave me and my family alone the rest of the time. Okay?'

The door was slammed again. Tammy was not watching from the window, but she had probably heard every word from wherever she was hiding in the house. I went back to the Austin and drove home, feeling more than a little deflated.

29

'What is it with your crazy kids and rats?' Arnold the bus driver said to me, the following week. He had come in to collect his wages, and seemed utterly perplexed. 'I drive a lot of kids to a lot of places, and I'd say I pass half a dozen rats every day,' he said. 'But I have *never* encountered children who get excited every time we come across one of the bloody rodents. What are you *teaching* them here?'

'Are they better behaved? Easier to manage?' I asked.

'They are, as it happens.'

'Then wouldn't you say a love of rats is a small price to pay?'

Arnold walked out thinking about that one.

I talked to my colleagues about the effect Samuel Whiskers was having on the kids during a break later that day.

'They're into rats now, apparently,' I said to Lonnie. 'How can we capitalize on *that*?'

'I know I'm small, but I do not know any rats,' Lonnie said stiffly. 'And I am offended at the suggestion.'

'Umm . . . I know a rat,' Tush said.

I looked pointedly at her. 'I'm not referring to ex-boyfriends here, or any solicitors or politicians you might know,' I said. 'I mean whiskered, long-tailed things that look like big mice.'

'I have a pet rat,' she said.

'Really?' I asked.

'Yes. Risso. I've had him since he was little.'

'What do you call a baby rat?' I asked.

'They're pups,' Tush said.

'You are full of surprises, aren't you?' I said.

'Do you feel comfortable bringing your pet in here with this bunch?' Susan said. 'Does . . . uh . . . Risso bite at all?'

'No, he's very tame,' Tush said. 'I think it'll be okay, so long as the children are gentle with him.'

'What if he escapes and takes up residence under the floorboards?' Lonnie said, shuddering. 'I don't want to get captured and turned into a pudding.'

'Are you a little rat-phobic, perhaps, my dear Alonzo?' I asked.

'I'm just being practical,' Lonnie said, but he skulked off looking unhappy.

The next day, Little Scamps had a visitor.

Tush kept him in her car until breakfast had been cleared away, then brought in his cage with a towel draped over it. 'I need you all to stay very quiet and not to make any sudden movements,' she said to the children. 'I have a friend in here I'd like you to meet.'

'Is it a fairy?' Mitzi asked.

'Is it a Smurf?' Ross asked. 'I bet it's a Smurf.'

Tush swept the towel away, and there, sitting on his hind legs and sniffing the air keenly, was a good-sized brown rat. The revelation was met with utter silence by the children, who didn't seem to realize at first what they were seeing.

'This is Risso the Rat,' Tush said. 'He's around two years old, which makes him quite old for a rat – he can probably live until he's three, so long as he doesn't get hurt or sick. He

179

is a Brown Rat, which means he is one of the most successful animals on the earth – did you know there are more brown rats on this planet than any other animal? Even people?'

The children were still completely silent, gazing fixedly at the cage and its occupant.

'Can you take him out, Tush?' Gus asked. 'I wants to see him.'

'No, leave it in its cage,' Milandra said. 'I don' like him. He's a fuckin' creepy animal. My dad says rats is dirty and has d'seases.'

'That's true, Milandra,' Tush said. 'Wild rats do carry some diseases that are quite nasty, and their fleas – little insects that live in their fur – can have horrible sicknesses on them too. But, you see, Risso has never been in the wild. He was born in a pet shop, and I was given him as a present when he was still a baby. I make sure he gets all his injections and that he never has fleas or worms in his tummy, or anything that might make him ill. It's quite safe to take him out and stroke him. But only if you want to.'

It was agreed by consensus that Risso would come out of the cage and that anyone who was afraid or uncomfortable could go outside with Lonnie (who volunteered for the task), while the others could play with him and ask more questions. Needless to say, Milandra, Mitzi and Julie chose to go out, while the boys and Tammy stayed to meet Tush's friend.

Risso proved to be as gentle as Tush had said he was. The children outdid themselves in gentleness, too. The rat was passed around without the remotest hint of anxiety or calls for anyone to hurry up, and Tush was asked some very interesting questions.

'What does he eat, Tush?' Gilbert said.

'Well, he'll eat almost anything,' Tush said. 'But he prefers things like sunflower seeds and corn. He *loves* cheese, but I wouldn't give it to him every day because he'd get fat.'

'Just like Samuel Whiskers!' Ross said.

'Just like that,' Tush said, keeping a watchful eye on how Risso was being handled.

'He brainy?' Jeffrey asked.

'Very,' Tush said. 'Rats are reckoned to be almost as clever as dogs. When rats live in the wild, they spend their time in groups, a bit like dogs do, and every rat has a role and a job. Rats look after one another – they clean each other, they play together and they're very clever at finding food. I've seen Risso there work out how to get the lid off a jar of nuts – it took him ten minutes or so to do it, but once he did it, he never forgot how. So he's really clever.'

The kids were allowed to play with Risso for about half an hour, then Tush decided it was time he went back into his cage.

'I'm going to leave him in the nature corner today,' she said. 'And I'm trusting you all to behave well around him. Risso is a living thing, so you have to be nice to him, just like you would to one another.'

We all got up from our chairs, and it was then that I saw Milandra standing in the doorway watching us.

'You shouldn' be havin' childrens playin' wit a dirty rat,' she called.

'We discussed this, Milandra,' I said, walking towards her so we wouldn't be shouting across the room. 'Risso is not dirty. You kids have been talking about rats since we had the story at Hallowe'en. This was a chance to learn about them.'

'I'm tellin' my daddy.'

'You do that,' I said. 'I have no problem with you telling your parents about anything we do here. There are no secrets at Little Scamps.'

I was purposely keeping my voice light and positive, even though I felt a coil of anger in my gut. From the moment I had met Milandra's father, I had known this would happen – that I would be played off against him. Where there are behavioural problems, it's essential that all adults show a united front around children. Displaying antagonism and discord leads to even greater problems.

'My daddy don't like you,' the child said. 'He says you *ôkùnrin ábökùnrinlò.*'

'I don't know what that means, Milandra,' I said. 'You know I don't speak Yoruba, sweetie.'

'Iss a bad name,' she said. 'D'you like my daddy?'

I had been waiting for this, too. I've experienced similar conversations with children whose parents had abused them. 'Do you think my daddy is a bad man for doing that to me?' is a common question, and one that carries a lot of risk if one is not forewarned. The last thing you want to do when dealing with a child who is already confused and numbed from physical or emotional turmoil is insult their parents, even where that parent hurts their child on a regular basis. Blood is a powerful bond, and even children who are being brutalized continue to love their parents. Sometimes the appropriate response requires some verbal contortion.

'I'm sure your daddy is a wonderful man,' I said, smiling warmly.

'You 'n' him fighted when you brunged me home that day,' Milandra said tersely.

'Yes, we had some words,' I said – she had been there, so there was no point in denying it, 'but I know he was worried about you so I'm not going to be hurt or upset about it.'

'He says you do bad work here.'

'He's entitled to his opinion,' I said. 'Come on, let's get ready for drama.'

She went with me to get the others, but I knew we were in for trouble. It was only a matter of time before it erupted.

I didn't have to wait long. Drama was usually a period of unbridled fun where the children were encouraged to let their imaginations run riot. In the beginning I had directed the action by suggesting a story or theme for the kids to improvise around, but within a fortnight they began arriving into the crèche with their own ideas and issues to explore, and I saw that the most sensible thing to do was let them at it.

Today, of course, they wanted to act out the story of Samuel Whiskers. Except now he was to be called Risso Whiskers, in honour of our guest.

'When we is done wit de practisin' Tush can take him over and sit him on her knee to watch us,' Rufus said. 'Would dat be okay, Tush?'

'I bet he'd love to see the play,' Tush said.

There was no need to rehearse for very long. Tom Kitten had been climbing up chimneys and discovering under-floor kingdoms almost every day since we had told the story, and copies of the pictures from the book had been stuck on the wall around the dress-up area like a story-board so the children could refer to them at their leisure.

The kids had made masks for themselves – rats, cats and a dog-face for John Joiner, who was depicted in the book as a terrier – and they used brown and grey pieces of material to denote fur, tied about their shoulders as cloaks.

They followed the *Tale*'s plot loosely, but the dialogue could get quite creative, and on more than one occasion Tom (usually played by Ross) produced an imaginary gun and effected his own escape in a manner Quentin Tarantino would have admired. During another performance Samuel Whiskers and Anna Maria (played by Gus and Mitzi) decided to abandon the idea of a pudding, and just roasted the poor kitten as he was, allowing no time for an escape, cutting the story short. But, as Mitzi pointed out, the baddies have to win *sometimes*.

Since Mitzi's vocal talents had emerged, songs were included in most activities. They bore little relevance to the action and tended towards 1960s pop – we were regularly treated to 'California Dreamin'' or 'San Francisco'. The other children were remarkably indulgent of her, and even tried to sing along, even though they had never heard any of these anthems of peace, love and understanding before.

Milandra made her move during Mitzi's solo. She had refused to get involved in the show, and was sitting between Tush and me, her arms folded across her chest in an almighty strop. Risso was perched on Tush's knee, to all intents and purposes watching the drama just like the rest of us, his little black eyes fixed on the performers, whiskers twitching merrily.

Milandra waited for Mitzi to finish today's musical choice, an utterly bizarre version of Bob Dylan's 'Mr Tambourine Man' (it was word perfect, but the melody meandered between nursery rhymes, traditional Irish jigs and reels). As the child went into her now customary curtsy, Tush let go of Risso, upon whom she had a gentle hold, to clap. It was at that moment that Milandra grabbed and threw him across the room.

It seems certain she intended to smash poor Risso against the wall, but luckily he fell short. Tush did not react for a second, seemingly stunned by such wanton cruelty, but Tammy did. She had been standing at the side of the performance area, a kitten mask crooked across her forehead. As Risso soared over her head, Tammy moved with uncanny speed, and was beside him as he crash-landed on the floor. Seconds later, she was standing beside Tush, the rat trembling in her hands.

'Thank you, Tammy,' Tush said. She took her pet and put him back in the safety of his cage.

'Okay, Missy,' I said to Milandra, taking her gently by the arm. 'You and I are going to have a little chat.'

'You take your fuckin' hand off me right now, *ôkùnrin ábökùnrinlò*!'

'I'm just making sure you come with me and that you don't make a dash for the door,' I said. 'And you *are* coming with me, Milandra. You can mark my words on that.'

I steered her into the office and sat her on the desk, so she could be seen from outside – I wasn't having her saying I hurt her or did anything inappropriate, and I wasn't at all confident that she was beyond making such allegations.

'Milandra,' I said. 'That was a really, really mean thing you just did. Tush brought in her pet today so you could see it and learn about something new. Whether you like Risso or not, he belongs to Tush and he is a live animal, who can be hurt and frightened. You had no right to touch him without her permission, and you *absolutely* had no right to throw him.'

'My daddy tole me a only good rat is a dead rat,' Milandra shouted. 'He said when he was growin' up if they seed a rat, they squished it.'

I put my head into my hands. How was I supposed to work with this child when my efforts were consistently thwarted? What could I say to her, when she was simply acting on the wishes of her father? I had no idea, but I did know that I had to do something. Whatever she was being taught to do at home, there were some basic rules and boundaries at Little Scamps. One of those was that everyone – even rats – was entitled to feel safe. Neither Milandra nor her father was permitted to compromise that.

'Tush explained very clearly to you, and I know you understood her, that Risso is not a wild rat, and therefore does not carry disease and is quite clean. Lots of people have pet hamsters, mice and gerbils, and they are all vermin, too, but I doubt you would have tried to kill one of those if Tush had brought one in.'

Milandra growled something in Yoruba, an expression of sheer hatred on her face.

'You can be angry with me all you like,' I said. 'One thing we are allowed in Little Scamps is to own our feelings. It's quite okay to be angry. It's not okay to hurt anyone, and that includes pets. Now, I want you to think about what you just did. I'm going to make a space for you in the main room – you won't be by yourself – and I want you to stay there until you feel you are able to join the group again without being mean or spiteful to anyone.'

'I ain't stayin' anywhere,' Milandra spat. 'You can' make me. I'll get loose an' I'll smash the place.'

'You won't, because I won't let you.'

'I fuckin' will, you sumbitch. I'll fuckin' kill you an' all those udder rotten ol' kids.'

I picked Milandra up and carried her, kicking and screaming a loud string of multilingual obscenity, into the main room. Holding her under my right arm, I used my left hand to place a chair in an unused corner by the front entrance. I sat her on it, then stayed while she made some futile attempts to bolt, first in one direction, then another.

'No,' I said. 'You're going to stay here until you're feeling better.'

'I won't! I fuckin' won't!'

She was practically hysterical. Finally she sat down on the chair, put her head on her knees and howled. I watched for a few minutes, then left her to rejoin the others.

'Time out?' Susan asked, referring to the method of behaviour management I was using. 'Didn't expect you to opt for that.'

'Why?' I asked, Milandra's screeches punctuating the normal chatter of the room like a fog horn.

'Not very politically correct,' she said. 'Smacks a bit of punishment, doesn't it?'

'I'm out of options,' I said, watching Jeffrey and Gus playing an elaborate game with the toy cars and the model town. I was vaguely aware that my own voice was getting just a bit shrill. 'I'm the first one to advocate reinforcing good behaviour rather than punishing bad, but what do you do when there isn't any positive behaviour to reinforce? I can't have her holding the place to ransom and then have a little chat with her in the hope she might decide to be nice. There have to be repercussions for her actions. And maybe by trying to talk her through what she's done wrong, we're actually rewarding her bad behaviour – we're giving her undivided, one-on-one attention every time she acts out. Maybe some time on her own might be what she needs. Oh, Su, I don't know. I'm struggling here.'

She gave me a hug and laughed – it seemed that Milandra's conduct had somehow made her feel a bit better: the child's reaction to *everything* was unreasonable.

'Welcome to the real world,' she said. 'There is no harm whatsoever in trying to do it like the textbooks say, but the time always comes when you have to go old school.'

I sighed and rubbed my eyes with the heel of my hand. 'So why do I feel like shit, then?'

'Because that's how it feels sometimes,' Susan said, and hugged me again. 'For what it's worth, I think you're doing the right thing. Maybe you will too, when you finish beating yourself up about it.'

I watched Milandra off and on for the rest of the day, but I should have been watching Tammy. In all the kerfuffle I had forgotten about her penchant for vengeance. She appeared to have taken Milandra's abuse of Risso as a personal affront. I was attending to a towering Lego construction with Jeffrey and Julie when I heard what sounded like two cage fighters going at it. Whirling about, I was in time to see Tammy bludgeoning Milandra to the floor. I remember thinking, *Milandra's twice the size of her!* But I didn't have time for more than that because Tammy was kicking her victim in the head.

Susan got to them first and picked Tammy up under her oxters – the child continued to kick the air, even after Susan had whisked her away. I picked Milandra up to see if she was okay, and received a smack in the ear.

'I'll fuckin' kill that little *bitch*!' Milandra howled.

'She's fine,' I said, putting her back in her chair, where she started to bawl again – I couldn't tell if it was in temper or misery. In retrospect, it was probably both.

I would love to be able to report that Milandra cried for a time and then came back into the group having learned something about herself.

Sadly, she didn't.

She screamed and screamed, then threw the chair at Julie, who happened to be walking past, almost taking the child's head off. Susan restrained her for half an hour, before letting her go and informing her that she could come and play when she felt ready. Milandra stayed where she was.

It should have occurred to me to take away the chair at that point and give her a beanbag instead, but I was engrossed in helping Arga and Gilbert paint a picture of Tom Kitten. And Milandra was very quiet for a while, so I assumed she had burned herself out and fallen asleep. I was wrong: she was plotting her next step.

Music – in a more organized forum than Mitzi's vocal

stylings – had become a regular part of the programme since I had introduced the ukulele and 'The Elephant Song'. The last period before lunch that day was music, and I tried to vary the instruments I brought in to keep the children's interest up. Today I had my mandolin, and the children were armed with percussion instruments we had made – mostly washing-up liquid bottles filled with lentils, rice, chick-peas and any other objects that made a loud rattling sound.

I'd found songs that either told a story or involved some form of progression worked best, so I had dusted off my collection of ballads and counting songs – anything that didn't involve death, adultery or incest, more difficult than you'd think with folk music.

I had, and by then it shouldn't have been a huge surprise, discovered that songs with a rural or agricultural bent resonated with the children, which gave me a focus in my search for material. Pete Seeger had released several albums of game and activity songs back in the 1950s, and I had found them incredibly useful.

On this occasion we were singing a song that had become a great favourite: 'Fox Went Out On A Windy Night'. It dates back to at least the fifteenth century (a manuscript containing the lyric and some baroque notation from that period survives in the British Museum), and tells the story of a wily old fox who heads into town to steal a farmer's geese and chickens. It has easy, repetitive choruses and plenty of characters for the children to enjoy, and as the story progresses, there are quiet sections (when the fox is in the pen with the birds), noisy ones (the farmer's wife leaping out of bed), sound effects (the farmer blowing his horn to alert the neighbours that a fox is on the prowl) and so on.

What I loved most about singing songs like this with the children was that they took them so seriously. While they were not all farmers' children, they all knew farmers and had heard adults discussing the threat foxes posed to the local chicken population. Here was another example, just like *Peter Rabbit* and *Samuel Whiskers*, of a story they could grasp very easily and get involved in.

So we were completely distracted when Milandra struck again.

When I was singing with the children I conducted them by giving directions. Once we had done a song two or three times, this was hardly necessary, but I did it anyway, because I enjoyed it. We had reached the verse:

> John he ran to the top of the hill,
> Blew his horn both loud and shrill.
> The fox said: 'I'd better flee with my kill,
> For he'll soon be on my trail-o, trail-o, trail-o.'
> The fox said: 'I'd better flee with my kill
> For he'll soon be on my trail-o.'

'He's running up the hill now,' I said, playing a tight tremolo on the mandolin to denote running footsteps. 'Show me how he'd run up as fast as he can.'

The kids – even Mitzi – jumped off their chairs and jogged on the spot, their home-made shakers giving off a great racket.

'All right, now he's blowing the horn – he wants to tell everyone that the old fox is on the loose and after their chickens and geese. Give me a loud, loud horn sound!' I moved to high G on the mandolin and bent the string, giving a whooping, wailing note.

The children all hollered – '*Aaaooooaaah*' – putting their cupped hands around their mouths and marching up and down like soldiers.

That was when Milandra chose to throw her chair through the glass panel of the front door.

With all the other noise that was going on, the sound of the glass shattering and the metal legs of the chair clattering on the floor outside shouldn't have been as loud as they were, but I jumped, Tush screamed and several children got such a fright they began to cry.

Milandra stood where she was, a look of victory on her face. 'Can I come back to the group *now*, you dirty fuckers?' she asked.

30

The crèche was empty. I sat in the silent space and wondered what in the name of all that was good and holy I, or any of us, could do to get through to Milandra. I felt I had failed her and the rest of the children, as well. Little Scamps had become a pleasant place to be of late, but out of the blue Milandra's rage had re-emerged, and it was not making for a very relaxed atmosphere. Gilbert in particular found such outbursts unnerving, and they brought out his latent violence, too. If we didn't do something to stem the flow of aggression, I would have no choice but to take drastic measures – like admitting that Milandra had us beat, and requesting that her parents remove her from Little Scamps.

That was a course of action I did not relish, mainly because I thought Milandra deserved better, but it also felt like I was admitting defeat to Tony. Hadn't he said that I couldn't control my charges? Maybe he was right.

As it was, we had decided it would be best for Susan and Lonnie to bring her home as, once again, she was not safe to put on the bus. We reasoned that my presence would just aggravate things. I hoped Lonnie would give Tony a run for his money if they encountered one another.

There was a knock on the door.

Who the hell was this?

'Yeah, come in,' I called, unsuccessfully trying to hide the annoyance in my voice.

The door swung open and Tristan Fowler came in. 'Thought I'd drop by to see how you're doing.'

'I'm doing shit, thanks for asking,' I said.

'That good, eh?' my boss and friend mused.

'Yup.'

'Fancy a pint? Tell me all about it?'

'You're on,' I said.

Maybe I did want a little company after all.

I locked up and we drove to my place, parked the cars and went to my local. I talked about Milandra and her parents, the vitriol that seemed to hang about her, like a swarm of invisible insects – we couldn't see it, but the hum and vibration were definitely detectable.

Tristan considered my story. The pub was dark in the late winter evening, a fire burning in the hearth, a few people in for a quick glass of something on their way home from work. We each had pints of Guinness in front of us. I wanted a cigarette, but not so badly I would have killed for one. Which was an improvement.

'What did I tell you about social-care work back when we first met?' Tristan asked.

'You told me lots of things,' I said. 'You need to be more specific.'

'You can't approach any problem head on,' Tristan said, pretending I had not spoken. 'People – children – they're not like that. You have to think your way around some kind of corner, most of the time.'

'How do I do that with Milandra?' I asked. 'She tends to favour the head-on approach, as far as I can see.'

Tristan took a deep swallow of his stout. 'Does she? Do you think her actions today were *really* about rats? Come on, man – you've more sense than that.'

'So what were they about, then?'

'Okay, let's treat it like a jigsaw puzzle. Help me to examine the pieces. What do we know about Milandra?'

I counted the details on my fingers – they didn't amount to much. 'She's five years old. Her mother, Felicity, is Irish, blond, very pretty, works part-time in an estate agent's, as far as I know. Her dad, Tony, is Nigerian and is an executive at some sort of global communications company. Milandra speaks three languages I know of, but seems to favour her African heritage and Yoruba. I always get the feeling she speaks English to us because she has to. She has formed no real attachments at Little Scamps – if I had to name one person she looks to more than any other, I'd say Susan, but it's a matter of degrees. Her parents seem to dote on her, although I got the impression Felicity is worn out with her, and that Tony might be encouraging her behaviour – he called her his "warrior" when I brought her home, as if he was praising her for raising hell. I was prepared to accept that her strop had been down to low self-esteem before that, but since meeting her parents and seeing how they are with her, I'm not so certain.'

Tristan nodded. 'It's a complex one,' he said. 'Let's try and break the issue down into its component parts. First, there could be a cultural element.'

'She's Irish, Tristan,' I said. 'Even speaks Gaeilge fluently, for God's sake.'

'You tell me her dad is raising her very much as an African princess. That her wish was to have a doll in her own image. I did some work in the UK among recent immigrants from

Yoruba villages. Among their culture the most important thing is the survival of the parents, as the family – meaning the children – cannot survive without the parents being healthy. Often they will get the lion's share of whatever food is available, to the detriment of the children. What if, in this instance, Tony is putting Milandra into the alpha female role, subjugating the mother, giving the child an unbalanced sense of entitlement?'

I was confused. 'Why would he do that? It doesn't make sense in light of what you've just said.'

'Because the child is so obviously his descendant. Felicity is white – she's even blond, for God's sake. Milandra is his line, the sign of his virility, his masculine power. The Yoruba value strength and dominance. He's encouraging her to display that. She has learned to try to instil fear in those around her. What did Tony do when he met you? He went into your personal space, used his height to intimidate you.'

'It worked!' I laughed. 'Look, all you've confirmed for me is that Milandra is learning her behaviour at home. That, my friend, is not cultural. I've known plenty of white parents encourage their children to be little shits. It still leaves me with the same question: how do I overcome the learned behaviour so she'll settle down in the crèche?'

'She's of normal intelligence, you say, maybe even above normal.'

'I think so.'

'Okay. What it comes down to is how well Milandra can understand the situation she's in. At her age, she bases her concept of how she should behave on the conduct she sees around her. A five year old relies heavily on what she sees her parents and the significant adults in her life doing.'

'And her parents are *the* most important significant adults in her life,' I shot back.

'Yes indeed, but as her care workers, you spend a huge amount of time with her. Some theorists, people like Piaget, for example, suggest that teachers can greatly influence a child's moral development by giving them tasks that offer a chance to solve various problems and reach useful answers, rather than trying to indoctrinate them with patterns of behaviour. Get them to do the work for themselves, in other words.'

Jean Piaget was a Swiss psychologist who had massively influenced our understanding of children's intellectual development.

'I thought I'd been doing that,' I said. 'We've been doing loads of activities that look at moral issues and discussing the ins and outs of them – hence all the Beatrix Potter stuff.'

Tristan thought that one over. 'Fair enough. Maybe your problem, then, is that Milandra doesn't see herself as one of the group. Why should she adopt your code of behaviour if she isn't really one of you?'

I couldn't argue with that. It was something I had considered but I had been unable to find a suitable way to address.

'We've gone out of our way to make her welcome in the group,' I said. 'The birthday party was just one example. I can't think of anything we haven't done.'

'Maybe you're over-compensating,' Tristan said. 'If you treat her *too* nicely, single her out, it may make her feel even more vulnerable. Can you think of a piece of work that might involve the whole group, but still has individual pieces of activity, that might instil a sense of place and belonging for everyone?'

I knew he had something in mind. 'Tell me.'

He did. And I thought it just might work.

31

I stood in Mulligan's, a small supermarket and the main grocery store in the village, with Julie, Arga and Gilbert. The manager, a fat, moustachioed man in a suit that almost hid his outrageous paunch, was telling the children how long there had been a sales outlet at this location. Julie stood quietly, holding my hand, her tiny frame wrapped in a dark brown duffel coat. Gilbert, his blond curls encased in a red woolly hat with a white tassel, held my other hand. Arga was on Gilbert's other side.

'So, you see, there have been Mulligans in this village, on this very spot, selling reasonably priced groceries and select hardware products to the good people of Brony for nearly one hundred years.'

Arga started to clap uncertainly so we all joined in. Mr Mulligan beamed from ear to ear, which made him look like a happy panda.

'Do you know, I had no idea there was a school for handi— – for special – for children like that in the village?' Mulligan said, as he walked us out.

'Oh, yes,' I said. 'It's very hard for parents to find a child-care place for kids with unusual requirements. What usually happens, like in the case of Little Scamps, is that the health services set up places specifically to deal with that need.'

'Well, I think it's a wonderful idea,' the large man said, beaming. 'Aren't they lovely little kids? And so well mannered.'

'Mmm. They're on their best behaviour, right now, but yes, they're great,' I said, grinning down at the trio of angelic faces.

'You know, I had a cousin with – what d'you call it? He was like that little girl there.'

'Down's syndrome,' I said.

'That's it. Sure it was a long time ago – I'm nearly sixty, would you believe?'

I would have believed it, but I feigned surprise.

'Well, he was around the same age as me. I used to play with him when my aunt came to visit. We were great friends. Then one day he was gone. I didn't find out till years later that they'd put him in a home. I never saw him again.' The big man looked at Julie with a soft expression. I could tell he was a long way away, recalling a childhood friendship cut brutally short. 'You call in any time,' he said, slapping me on the back so hard he nearly winded me. 'And bring your friends there. If I can help you in any way, don't hesitate to ask. Mulligan's Groceries and Hardware Supplies has always been to the fore in helping out the local community.'

I thanked him and led the children across the street. I held up my phone, which had a fairly basic camera, and clicked a photo of the shop's façade. Then I squatted so I was at the kids' level.

'I want you all to get a really good picture of the shop in your heads,' I said. 'Where is it on the street, first of all?'

'*Blisko pub, obok apteki*,' Arga said. 'Near pub, next to . . .' She stopped, trying to find the word. '. . . chemist.'

'That's right. And what colour is the outside?'

Julie pointed to her trainers, which were bright yellow. The colours weren't an exact match, but they were close.

'Absolutely,' I said, high-fiving her. 'It's yellow. And where is Little Scamps from here? How do we get back to it?'

Gilbert turned to look back down the street. 'That way,' he said, pointing.

'How far is it?' I asked. 'How long would it take me to find my way there?'

'Short,' he said. 'Short time to get there.'

'Would it be as long as, say, an episode of *Zach and Cody*?' I asked, referring to a kids' show of thirty minutes duration that they all watched. When children have only a cursory sense of time, it's good to have something they can easily grasp to compare it to.

'No. Not that long,' Gilbert said.

'All right, then, would it be as long as the ad break in the middle of *Zach and Cody*?'

This was around three minutes, by my reckoning, and would tally with about how long we would have to walk if we went fairly slowly, and the kids rarely walked fast unless it was to get to the bathroom or to eat something.

'Yeah, that long,' Gilbert said, a vague smile breaking across his strange, beautiful face.

'Well done, you lot,' I said, getting the three of them in a group hug. 'I'd like you all to remember everything we've learned, because I want you to put it all into the amazing map we're going to make. Your part is going to be Mulligan's Store, and I want it to be just the best, most amazing work you can do. You gonna do that for me?'

'Yeah!'

We held hands again and began the short walk back to Little Scamps.

All of the children made similar journeys about the village that day, and every single shop, the butcher's, the barber's, the post office, and the two pubs were visited by representatives from our crèche. The reactions were universally the same: the business owners had had no idea of our existence, and seemed genuinely touched that we had bothered to call on them as part of our latest project. Quite a few had stories similar to Mr Mulligan's, and everyone invited us back and offered help and support should we need it. The children were viewed as wonderful additions to the village (even though more than half of them came from a good distance away), and I detected a real sense of pride that Brony was home to such a specialist establishment: other villages or towns might cast out such needy children, but Brony took them to her bosom.

That might or might not have been true, but I thought it a trifling concern. The reality was that our kids had been welcomed with open arms, and they had seen it with their own eyes. More importantly, *Milandra* had seen it. I wanted her not only to feel a sense of belonging and solidarity with everyone else at Little Scamps, but to experience real pride in the crèche. If she was her daddy's African warrior princess, it might appeal to her to be part of such an exclusive group.

The project we were mounting was one I had done and enjoyed while working with Tristan at Drumlin. It was all about getting to know not just your community but your place in it. We would make a huge, colourful map of the village, depicting every shop, house and feature, including Little Scamps, and make them as lifelike as possible. Each child would take responsibility for one building in particular, but we would all help – the point of the task was for us to work as a team, learn about our local environment, and one another.

In Drumlin, where the client group were adults, the project had lasted almost a month, and the end result was almost photo-realistic. Susan, Tush, Lonnie and I were under no illusions that that would *not* be the case at Little Scamps. We endeavoured to make the process as easy as we could, so we produced coloured card and recommended using as much collage material as possible. In that way we could move the task along without boring anyone.

The children, however, proved to be perfectionists.

'That ain't right,' Ross said, looking at the image of the local pharmacy.

I had the relevant photo on the computer monitor so the kids could refer to it, and Ross was leaning on his crutches, looking from the screen to the paper creation we had spread out on the floor. I had suggested the green walls of the building might be re-created using spinach *farfalle* pasta, stuck on with paste. The children seemed open to this suggestion, and the stiff paper had been smeared with glue and the dried pasta liberally tossed on. But Ross, who was co-ordinating this piece of the map, was unhappy.

'What's the problem, Ross?' I asked.

'Look at dat pitcher,' Ross said, pointing at the screen with his crutch.

'Yeah?' I said.

'The walls are ... like ... smooth. These're bumpy 'n' lumpy.'

I looked at our work, then at the digital image. He was right. 'What d'you want to do, Rossie?'

'All that stuff is gonna have to come off,' he said.

Milandra wandered over. 'Whatcha doin'?' she asked.

'Oh, no,' Ross moaned. 'Have you come to wreck everything now, M'landra?'

I winced. We didn't need one of her legendary rages.

'I'm only askin',' she said.

'All righ',' Ross said. 'The walls is all wrong. We done 'em wit dat passghetti stuff, but it's too wobbly.'

Milandra considered the problem. 'Maybe you could smash it all down. Then it'd look hard, but it wouldn't be stickin' up.'

'I don' know,' Ross said, obviously uncertain. 'You always like smashin' stuff. I don' wanna wreck my buildin'.'

I left them to it – this was a problem that was within their grasp to resolve, and it was fascinating to watch them sort through the options.

'You won't wreck it,' Milandra said. 'You want to take 'em all off anyways. If you don' like it, you c'n still take 'em off. We just has to be careful not to rip de paper, 's all.'

Ross looked at me for confirmation. I shrugged. 'Can't hurt, Ross. I'll help you get all the pasta off if you still don't like it.'

Ross chewed his lower lip, moving around the piece of paper, which was almost as big as him.

'How should I smash 'em?' he asked Milandra.

'Jus' walk over 'em'd be the quickest way.'

Ross raised a crutch to move on to the piece of art, then stopped. 'I'll rip it if I go on there. My sticks'll do it, I know they will.'

'We can fix it,' I said. 'We can just tape down any tears. Don't worry. You go ahead.'

'No.' Ross shook his head firmly. 'I put a lotta work into this. We all did. I'm not gonna rip it. You do it, M'landra.'

She shot him a look of utter surprise. The children never trusted her to do anything: she was never offered a toy that she had not snatched or stolen, never invited to join a game without having barged in. This was new territory for her. 'You *really* want me to do this for you?'

Ross seemed to be reconsidering his suggestion. I prayed he would hold firm, but I knew I had to keep my mouth shut. There was delicate work going on here – far too fragile for me to interfere with.

'Yeah. Yeah, okay. You do it – but go carefully, right? Will you do that, M'landra?'

She seemed to swell with pride and delight. 'I surely will, Rossie boy. Watch me smash those pastas for ya. You keep an eye on me, now – this is your bit of de project, isn't it?'

You may have heard the phrase 'walking on eggshells'. That was exactly what came to mind as I watched Milandra tiptoe about Ross's picture, gently crushing the pasta so that it looked like a thin membrane of green concrete, a spider web of filigreed cracks running throughout. It took her a good five minutes to do the whole thing, and I could see the strain in her as she maintained her concentration – she had promised Ross she would do this for him, and she was not going to let him down.

When she had finished, I lifted her off the page and we all looked down. Ross was grinning like a Cheshire Cat. 'It's just right!' he said, to Milandra, with genuine warmth. 'Look what you done, M'landra – it's *perfect*! It looks like real stone, that wall does.'

'It really does,' I said, lifting the paper and shaking off the loose bits of pasta so that we were left with the clean, completed piece. 'Good job, guys.'

'Yeah, well, I did that for you, Ross,' Milandra said gruffly. 'You needed some help, and I done it.'

'Thanks,' Ross said, putting a hand on her shoulder.

'Tha's what friends do for one 'nother,' Milandra said.

'Well, if you need help with your bit, just ask me,' Ross said eagerly.

Milandra looked at him. I could see her mind working.

A week ago, she would have cut off her right arm before allowing anyone to help her with anything. I waited for her response with bated breath.

'I think I do need a little bit of help,' she said, 'if you'd like to help me.'

And off the pair went.

The trip about the village in the cold – and often wet – weather meant the children needed plenty of outdoor wear, and a change of clothes in case they were caught in a downpour. I – and the other staff agreed with me – was of the opinion that the elements should never be an excuse not to take the children outside. When we engaged in projects like the map, we sent notes home to the parents, asking them to make sure their child arrived in with the gear and equipment they needed, and all responded by doing just that. All except Tammy's parents, Kylie and Dale.

The main work of going around to visit each store was done over one day, but the process of building the village in two dimensions took longer, and required the children be able to pop outside to have another look at the subject of their creativity. Tammy arrived in on the first day with her usual weathered T-shirt and jeans combo. There was no way we could allow her out into the elements dressed so flimsily, so I dug a battered anorak out of our emergency clothes bank and put it on her. By day three when, despite one more note being sent home, she still arrived improperly attired, I decided it was time to create a storage unit especially for Tammy – 'The Tammy Cupboard'. In it we kept clothes, a lunchbox and whatever other bits and pieces she needed. It meant we always had something to hand.

I was surprised to discover that Tammy knew exactly where the source of her emergency items was. One day we were going on a nature walk and the other children were putting on their wellingtons. When I arrived at the Tammy Cupboard, she was already there waiting for me, her grey sneakers off and an expectant expression on her face.

Something unexpected happened in relation to Tammy around this time, something I took to be a huge leap forward. It involved little Julie.

Julie was the smallest child in the group, and was generally sweet natured and slow to anger. While some of the kids treated her with a degree of deference because of her apparent meekness, she was often the butt of practical jokes, bullying and general ill treatment. Lonnie, Tush, Susan and I kept an eye on her to make sure she was okay, while at the same time encouraging her to stand up for herself. Little Scamps was not a place for the shy or retiring: it was very much governed by survival of the fittest.

As the map was being completed there was great competition for materials and art equipment, and the children were constantly snatching odds and ends when they thought their owners weren't watching, or forcibly removing them if they were. Julie was particularly vulnerable to such assaults.

Unfortunately, even with our best intentions, we could not keep her under scrutiny every single second – and the moment our eyes were elsewhere, the opportunity was taken.

Julie had been using a pot of bright purple paint to colour the flowers in a window box of the flat above the supermarket. Rufus wanted purple paint to finish off a car he was placing on the roadside near the pub. He could, of course, have waited the fifteen minutes it would have taken Julie to finish, but patience had never been Rufus's strong suit. Without a word, he walked up, took the paint from her hand, and went back to where he was working. Julie looked surprised for a moment, then went to take it back. Rufus pushed her over. Julie began to wail.

And Tammy stepped in.

It all happened very quickly. She walked briskly over from where she had been working and punched Rufus straight in the forehead. He keeled over backwards and Tammy caught the paint pot as he went down. She helped Julie up and handed her the purloined item, patting her gently on the head before going back to what she had been doing.

It was the beginning of a new role for Tammy as Julie's stalwart protector. I had known her to help Gilbert from time to time, but I often thought that had more to do with the piercing cry he could emit when upset – Tammy comforted him or came to his assistance to stop him screeching. She had never expressed any interest in Julie before, yet over the next week barely a day went past without her rushing to the smaller child's aid. Very quickly the other kids started to leave Julie alone, or even to ensure that she was all right, such was their fear of Tammy's ire.

'What do you think it means?' Tush asked me one evening, as we watched Tammy leading Julie out to the bus, the two girls hand in hand.

'If I weren't so hardened and cynical, I'd say Tammy has made a friend,' I said.

'But why Julie?'

'She's little, quiet, needs looking after – I'd say that, other than Gilbert, she's the least threatening kid in the crèche, wouldn't you?'

'Why would she want someone who isn't threatening? Everyone else here is scared of her.'

'If, as we suspect, Tammy's problems are about being rejected, well, which kid is least likely to reject her?'

'Julie,' Tush admitted.

We watched the pair climbing up the steps of the bus, Tammy, tiny as she was, helping the even littler Julie.

'Kind of sweet, though, isn't it?' I asked.

'You soppy git.' Tush laughed, and went to clean up.

We hung the map in the entrance hallway. Though it was nowhere near as accurate and artfully done as the equivalent in Drumlin, I thought it a thing of remarkable beauty. The kids adored it. I made a point of popping around to all the shopkeepers and businesses in the village to tell them it was completed and on display and, to my delight, a good many dropped in to see their premises immortalized in poster paint, bits of wool and lollipop sticks. The children took great pride in explaining how they had gone about creating their particular representation of the shop, pub or office, and then we offered our visitor a cup of tea.

My favourite aspect of the map, though, was seeing how the children used it. I hadn't intended this – it happened naturally.

One Monday I noticed that Gus, Arga and Milandra were missing. Hearing little voices deep in conversation, I followed them to the entrance hall. There the three were, leaning against the wall, gazing up at the map.

'We wented into the supermarket first,' Gus said, pointing at Mulligan's on the wall, 'then I asked my mammy if I could have a cake, so she tooked me into Kate's and she had a cup of tea.'

'I go Kate's too,' Arga said. 'My daddy like cake with carrot in it.'

'Carrot cake,' Milandra said. 'You call it carrot cake. I think it's shit.'

'Shit bad word,' Arga said matter-of-factly. 'Carrot cake bad cake.'

'I never been to Kate's,' Milandra said. 'I might ask my mammy to bring me one day.'

'Kate's café is nice,' Gus said. 'Kate is big and fat and her belly shakes when she laughs.'

'Kate give nice hugs,' Arga said.

'Nice hugs,' Milandra said. 'It'd be good to get one of those.'

'Time to come in for breakfast and news,' I said. Then I added: 'But there's no rush. Take your time.'

I reckoned the work that was going on out there was just as important.

32

It was a Saturday in early December. I fancied getting out, listening to some good music and having a few drinks. I also figured that a change of scene wouldn't do any harm. I called Lonnie.

'How'd you fancy heading to Dublin for the night? Have a few pints, catch a gig, maybe?'

'Sounds like a plan. You driving?'

'I can do that.'

'Maybe I should get the bus, then.'

Dublin was a-bustle with early Christmas shoppers. I booked us rooms in Brooks Hotel on Drury Street. Justin Townes Earle, son of the great Steve Earle, was playing in Vicar Street and we managed to get some last-minute tickets. The gig was wonderful: Earle is a tremendously talented singer-songwriter and a brilliant guitarist who takes his craft very seriously. He was in flying form. Taking to the small stage alone with his guitar, he treated us to more than two hours of his songs of lost love and hard living, and threw in plenty of stories about his exploits while under the influence of far too many chemicals for one man to have imbibed and still be alive.

When the gig was over Lonnie and I repaired to a nearby hostelry to have a few beverages before turning in for the night.

'That kid is one cool cookie,' Lonnie said. 'What a life.'

'He's something all right,' I agreed. 'He's ten years younger than me, but he's certainly covered a hell of a lot more ground.'

Lonnie favoured bottled beer, and he was sipping some kind of American stuff that I thought tasted a bit like fizzy water and had about as much kick.

'Makes me feel like a bit of a sissy,' he said. 'I mean, I'm more than forty, and what have I got to show for it?'

'Shit, Lonnie, I don't know,' I said. 'You've got a house with no mortgage, a job you love – don't tell me you don't – and a girl who happens to think you're pretty damned amazing. That's not a bad place to be, if you ask me.'

'Will you stop going on about Tush?' Lonnie said. 'That's never going to go anywhere.'

'Why the hell not? She's into you – and I know she is because I asked her – and you're into her. What more do ye need?'

Lonnie drained his bottle and went to the bar for another. When he sat down he looked out of the window at the people milling back and forth on Dame Street. 'This is the first time I've been in Dublin since I left that school I told you about.'

I hadn't known that. 'Welcome back, then.'

He laughed. 'Guess how many girlfriends I've had.'

'I'm no good at guessing games,' I said.

'Humour me.'

'Okay – five?'

'Lower.'

'Three?'

'Lower.'

210

'One?'

'Lower.'

I blinked. 'Oh. I'm sorry, man.'

'I am, quite literally, the forty-year-old virgin, only I'm actually more than forty. I'm fucking pathetic. Tragic. How am I ever going to approach a girl like Tush, who has everything going for her? She could be with any guy she wanted.'

'She wants *you*, Lonnie. That's the thing. Why can't you just accept that and be happy? You're being given a real chance here!'

'I don't know. Every time I try to imagine us together as a couple, it just doesn't fit. What would people say?'

I almost choked on my Guinness. 'Am I fucking hallucinating? Lonnie Whitmore worrying what other people might say about him?'

'I don't mean *people* – I mean, like, her parents and that. Can you imagine me being brought home to meet Mum and Dad? They'd have a heart attack.'

'See, this is your problem,' I said. 'You over-think everything. She's not talking about marrying you, mate. She just wants to go out for a bite to eat, have a drink, maybe, see a movie. Would it be so weird for you to let your guard down and just have some fun once in a while?'

'Maybe it is,' Lonnie said. 'Maybe I don't know how.'

'Well, you'd better learn fast,' I said. 'Because life is going to pass you by, and you'll still be stuck in your little house on the mountain, with it falling down around your fucking ears, all by yourself. How do you like the sound of that?'

'Millie would still love me,' he said.

'She really *isn't* the smartest dog in the world,' I agreed.

33

Making the map had achieved what we'd hoped, and given the children of Little Scamps a feeling of place and a sense of belonging. They were, without doubt, and for the first time, a unit. Christmas was to cement the new status quo in ways I could never have foreseen.

The children were as excited about the approaching holiday as any other kids. The walls were hung with posters and images of Santa Claus, reindeer and sleigh-bells, and Arga insisted we get a tree. This was no great difficulty as Rufus's dad, Bill, sold them from the back of a truck near the south end of the village. We all trooped down and there was great discussion about which was the most appropriate one for us. When the correct one was chosen – a surprisingly poor specimen, with huge patches devoid of foliage – Bill flatly refused to accept any payment.

'Never would've sold that one anyway,' he said. 'Sorry-lookin' yoke.'

'That's why we want it,' Ross said. 'It's just right for us. We'll make it look better. Wait and see!'

The effort that was put into decorating the tree was something to behold. Arga declared that there were to be no decorations bought, we had to make all of them ourselves. We spent two days making paper chains, baking star-shaped gingerbread cookies, shredding tin-foil into our own glitter and cutting out cardboard angels, Santas and presents for the kids to colour in.

When Gus and Arga, who seemed to be managing the decoration process, declared that there were enough adornments on the tree, Milandra noticed that there wasn't an angel on top. 'Ya gots t' have an angel, everyone knows that,' she said.

'Don't got one,' Jeffrey said. 'Want . . . me . . . draw . . . one?'

Tammy went to the toy box. She returned with Old Man Bear, the oldest and most beloved toy in the crèche, which Mitzi had once considered decapitating. 'Look what Tammy's got,' Milandra said. 'Here's our angel. Can we make clothes and wings for him?'

The kids all agreed that Old Man Bear was, indeed, an ideal angel, and Susan thought she might be able to sew some beautiful clothes and wings for him. Tammy was soon glowing with all the praise she got for her idea.

By home-time that evening, the tree had its angel. And it was, without doubt, the most perfect tree for our group.

The Kindness Box was still a weekly feature of the children's lives – something we now did on a Friday evening rather than every day, but still an item on the timetable to be looked forward to. There were usually only three children who wrote notes themselves: Milandra, Rufus and Ross. Gus could manage bits and pieces of writing, but nothing too challenging. Good deeds suggested by the other children had to be scribed by the staff, and after three or four readings of the box's contents, I was able to recognize the etchings of each calligrapher.

It came as a surprise when, one Friday near Christmas, I found a note in a strange hand among the others. It read, in a very neat but very tiny script: 'Rufus – for making a lovely card for his friend.'

I read the note to the group, and they applauded Rufus, who smiled and nodded, humility seeping from every pore.

'Who did you make the card for, Rufus?' I asked.

'He made one for all of us,' Milandra said. 'We all gots one.'

'Oh,' I said. 'Who wrote this note, then?'

Shrugs and head shakes all around.

'Someone must have written it,' I said.

Still no one claimed it.

I never found out who wrote that note – but I did see Tammy sitting in the corner, gazing at a home-made Christmas card. It was only later that it occurred to me that it might have been the only thing anyone gave her that year.

Christmas is my favourite time of year – I'm an absolute sucker for everything that goes along with it. Generally I'm a musical snob, but at Christmas I tune into a cheesy station that plays carols and novelty Christmas pop non-stop, and listen pathologically. I believe that the true smell of fellowship and good cheer is the aroma of mince pies baking in the oven. I can't get enough of it. In the complex world of childcare, however, Yuletide brings complications and difficulties. One of the problems wears a red suit and pilots a sleigh drawn by magic reindeer.

The profound philosophical issue Santa poses for some childcare workers is the inherent deception central to his existence. The bitter truth is that there is no merry old elf flying at super-human (or should that be super-reindeer?) speed across our skies delivering presents on Christmas Eve. Many of our children get precious little in their stockings, and I'm always hyper-aware of that when discussing the Father Christmas myth. The expectation Santa fosters can be undeniably cruel. Yet there is also something irresistibly beautiful about the image. He is the universal personification of goodwill and charity. Some bemoan the loss of spirituality from the Christmas season – I find myself welcoming it. Not the ludicrous, orgiastic spending, but the democracy it creates: Santa *should* be non-denominational. Too many children of all races and creeds need him. If that has somehow sped Christmas towards the consumerist hell it has become, then so be it.

The biggest issue I have with Kris Kringle, however, is my oath never to lie to children. About anything. This came to a head at Little Scamps as December wound towards its inevitable conclusion. Susan pulled me aside as I was laying out the breakfast things one morning, looking anxious.

'I got a call from Jeffrey's mother last night,' she told me. 'Apparently Mitzi told him there was no Santa during the bus ride home. He was very upset, but she's managed to talk him down. We're going to have to have a word with Mitzi. If the news gets out, we'll have a riot on our hands.'

'Mitzi's been a lot better lately,' I said. 'I'm sort of surprised at her.'

'In this instance, I blame her parents,' Susan said. 'Fucking hippies are so right on, they don't even want to observe Christmas. When I called them about it, they informed me that, as far as they're concerned, the season of goodwill is all a capitalist scam, designed to anaesthetize the masses.'

'They're entitled to their opinion,' I said. 'They might even be right.'

'You can't go around wrecking every other kid's childhood because of some wacky left-wing nonsense you're enamoured with,' Susan snapped, and went to get the cereal bowls.

The conversation began almost as soon as we had sat down for breakfast. Jeffrey was in high dudgeon, obviously feeling badly treated. Mitzi was uncharacteristically in a foul mood too. She usually hid her darker emotions under a sickly blanket of simpers and smiles. Not today.

'Me talk,' Jeffrey said, raising his spoon as soon as we were settled.

'Go ahead, Jeff,' Tush said. 'What's on your mind?'

'Mitzi hurt me,' he said.

'Did she?' Tush said. 'Mitzi, do you want to tell us what happened?'

'I did nothing,' she said, looking quite hurt herself. 'You say such bad things, Jeffrey the mongoloid. Bad, bad words.'

'That's a bad word, Mitzi,' Tush said. 'We do not use words like that at Little Scamps.'

'You. Fat!' Jeffrey said, jabbing his finger at her. 'Tell me no Santy.'

This last statement caused furore. All the children started speaking at once. I had to bang my spoon against my juice glass to get some order, and even then Gus continued to shout at Mitzi.

'Gus, you have to wait your turn,' I said. 'Jeff is speaking now, and Mitzi deserves the chance to tell her side too.'

'Her tell me no Santy,' Jeffrey said again. 'Make me cry.'

Mitzi was playing with her breakfast. She had lost a lot of weight in the past few months and, though still overweight, was nowhere near the size she had been when I'd first met her. Her overall conduct had improved considerably, too, the casual sadism more or less disappearing. It was as if her instinctive musical flair had given her an identity – she didn't need food to lift her spirits any more.

'Mitzi, did you tell Jeffrey that?' I asked.

'My mam and dad say that,' Mitzi said. 'They say, "Mitzi, we don't go for that crap." No Father Christmas. No presents. Christmas Day same as any other.'

'And it is quite all right for your mam and dad to believe that if they want to,' I said. 'But Jeffrey's parents believe something different, and it's also fine for them to celebrate Christmas and enjoy it in their way.'

'There *is* really a Santa, isn't there, Shane?' Gus asked, looking at me with such worry and apprehension that I was frozen to the spot.

Here was the question, the one I had been dreading. To lie or not to lie.

'Well, isn't it nice to think so?' I said carefully, hating myself for using such cheap news-speak.

'My older brudder tolded me there wasn't no Santy, and my mam shouted at him good,' Gus said sadly, picking up his toast. 'But I wondered about it since then. What if there isn't?'

'What do you want to believe?' Susan asked him. 'In your heart, what do you think is the truth?'

'I think it's true,' Ross said. 'I even think I heard him once, the sound of them bells. I was half asleep, 'cause I tried to stay awake to get a look at 'im. Think I nearly did, too.'

'I went to see him in the toy shop,' Milandra said. 'He smelt of cigarettes. I don' tink it was the real Santa.'

'Them ones in the shops ain't real,' Gus said. 'Even I know that.'

'Him real!' Jeffrey said, almost hyperventilating with fury. 'Mammy says!'

'You know how we decorated the tree?' I asked.

Nods.

'And you know how we've been singing carols and Christmas songs? And they make us feel so good and happy? Even Mitzi?'

More nods.

'And how we've read lots of Christmas stories and poems?'

217

All eyes were on me.

'For me, Christmas is about those feelings. It's a time when people are all just a little bit nicer to one another. It's a time when we all want to be with our families and the people we love, and when we try to think of how we can make those people really happy. And Santa is the person who we think of when we feel that way.'

'Christmas is baby Jesus's birfday,' Milandra said. 'My daddy said.'

'Yes, it's the time we celebrate Jesus's birthday,' I said. 'And any of us who are Christian should be thinking about that, too. But I reckon most people, for right or wrong, think of Santa first.'

'He's right, y'know,' Gus said, shaking his head like a little old man.

'Now, if so many people can act better, and if this time of year makes us do good things, and feel warm inside, then I'm happy to believe in Santa, and in magic,' I said.

'So you believe in him, then?' Gus asked hopefully.

'I do,' I said.

And it wasn't a lie.

I decided to take one last stab at Tammy's parents. I had drawn a complete blank with Kylie, so I decided to take Fiona Thomson's advice and see if I might not be able to open up some sort of line of communication with Dale. He was a mystery to me. I had never really spoken to him and knew little about him other than that he had a moderate criminal record. Fiona had said he drank at a pub near the little estate where he lived, so one evening I took a spin out that way to see if I could find it.

As a musician, I'm reasonably familiar with most of the hostelries near where I live, and I had heard of the pub that had to be Dale's watering-hole – the Herring Gull – but had never been in there. It was a small, run-down place, set in the middle of nowhere. Dale must have walked the three and a half miles to it from his house – good for sobering him up afterwards, I supposed.

I parked the Austin in one of the spaces outside the pub and went in. It was around seven o'clock and there was only one elderly man sitting at the bar supping from a large bottle of Guinness. The barman, a bearded man in his early fifties, looked up as I entered, seemingly surprised to see a new face. I doubted he got much passing trade – this was a local pub, if ever there was one.

'I'll have a Coke, please,' I said. I noticed a dusty piano in the corner and flipped open the lid. It was reasonably in tune.

'Me da left that,' the barman said, bringing me over my drink. 'Hasn't been played in years.'

'Mind if I keep myself amused for a few minutes?' I asked. 'We always had an upright piano at home when I was growing up, and I miss it.'

'Can you play?' the barman asked. 'Every now and again one of the lads has one too many and starts clattering the keys, and it sounds bloody awful.'

I played a gentle sequence of jazz chords. 'That good enough for you?' I asked.

'Play on, young man,' he said, gesturing at the instrument. 'As it happens, there's no one to disturb in here just now, anyway.'

I'm not really a piano player. We did have an old Hohner upright in the living room when I was a kid, and I taught myself to vamp chords and knock out the odd melody, but it would be stretching the truth to say I'm accomplished. I enjoy messing about on the keys, though, and can usually get something approximating to music from my efforts.

Ten minutes later the barman came back with another Coke. 'On the house,' he said. 'You've a nice touch.'

'Thanks.' I grinned.

'What brings you in here, if you don't mind my asking?' he ventured. 'We don't get a lot of strangers, particularly of a Monday night.'

'I'm looking for someone, actually,' I said. 'Guy by the name of Dale?'

'Dale Seavers?'

'Yeah.'

'He'll probably be in for one or two soon enough. Friend of yours?'

'Sort of,' I said. 'What's he up to, these days? He working?'

'No. And it's a damn pity,' the barman said. 'He's a talented mechanic. There isn't a car on the road he can't take apart and put back together again better than what it was.'

'That a fact?'

'It is. You sit tight. He'll be in. Do you know "Sonny"?'

'I do indeed.'

I played the old ballad for him, and even sang one or two verses. We were just finishing when Dale came in, grinning from ear to ear to hear the music. The smile dropped from his face rapidly when he saw who was behind it. He turned tail straight away and went right back out the door.

'I thought ye were friends,' the barman said, but I was already running after Tammy's father.

'Dale, come on, man, I just want a quick chat,' I called.

He was heading up the road, his head bowed, hands deep in his pockets. He stopped, turned and stalked back towards me. 'What right have you to invade my privacy like this? This is my local, my place – don't you *ever* come here again, d'ya hear me?'

'I've tried going to your house, Dale,' I said. 'You're either not there or you're unavailable.'

'I'm lookin' for work,' he said. 'Goin' out of me fuckin' mind sittin' round the house with Kylie.'

'You're a mechanic,' I said.

'Who told you?'

'Idle gossip,' I said, smiling. 'I hear you're pretty damn good.'

'I am,' he said, pride starting to kick in.

A thought occurred to me. 'I've been getting a sort of knocking sound in my engine lately,' I said. 'Think you might take a look at it for me?'

Dale scowled. 'I don't want no fuckin' charity.'

'Listen, I'm not about to offer charity when it comes to my vehicle,' I said. 'I'm fairly particular about it.'

Dale looked over my shoulder at the Austin. 'That's yours?'

'1981 Austin Allegro, third series, mint condition, all original parts,' I said.

He walked past me and looked at it, a smile spreading across his face. 'You don't see many of these any more,' he said. 'How does she run?'

I unlocked the door and turned the ignition. The motor purred to life immediately.

'I don't hear no rattle,' he said.

I pushed my foot on the accelerator, and the banging could easily be heard.

'I'd say that's your drive shaft,' Dale said, his hand resting on the bonnet. 'But I'd have to have a quick look to be sure.'

I switched off the engine and popped the bonnet.

Dale reminded me of a musician in the way he touched the components of my car. As soon as he began to work on it, I knew my beloved Allegro was in good hands. I had a small tool kit in the back, but he told me any mechanic worth his salt should be able to work with a can of oil, a couple of screw-drivers and a wrench. He explained everything he did, and answered all my questions directly – I have very little mechan-ical ability but understood him easily. He was a good teacher.

'How'd you learn about cars?' I asked him.

'Me da was a builder, but he was one of those fellas who could fix anything. He taught me a lot, and when I was four-teen I got a part-time job over the summer in a garage his brother, my uncle, owned. That was that. I knew I'd found me a job. Left school as soon as I could.'

'Well, it's good when you find what you love to do. Lot of people never do.'

'Problem is most of the cars they're buildin' now don't run like this baby does. If there's somethin' wrong, you just plug 'em into a computer. Makes people like me sort of . . . obsolete.'

'I don't like modern cars,' I said truthfully. 'They've got no personality.'

'Well, I can't argue with that,' he said. 'There, I think that'll do it.'

He handed me back the screwdriver he'd been using.

'That's it?' I asked.

'Just needed tightenin' up.'

'How much do I owe you?'

'No. Thanks, but no. The chance to get me hands dirty and work on a little beauty like this – call it quits.'

'Can I buy you a drink, then?'

He pondered that for a second. 'All right. Seein' as how we're here.'

The barman seemed relieved to see we had settled our dif-ferences, and greeted us warmly. Dale took a pint of lager and I had another Coke.

'Dale, I don't want to cause another row,' I said.

'Don't then,' he said, with a hard expression.

'I'm concerned about Tammy.'

He sighed deeply and drank a huge gulp of his beer. 'So what do you want me to do?'

'Well, if you're not working, why not come in to Little Scamps now and again, spend some time with her?'

'I'm not even sure that girl is mine,' he said quietly.

'I see her in you,' I said. 'Very much, around the eyes.'

He nodded. 'Yeah. I've heard that before,' he said.

'So help me to help her. I think she's very bright. I've seen her make some real progress in the last few weeks. If she felt you were behind her, I think she might make that extra leap.'

Dale took another slug of his drink. 'When I was a kid,' he said, 'I remember an aunt, on me mother's side, having a baby that wasn't right. Handicapped, y'know?'

I nodded.

'I remember me da takin' me aside and tellin' me that we would not be mentionin' that particular cousin. "There are no spastics or dullards in this family," he told me. This man was my da – my hero, understand?' Dale said.

I nodded again.

'My ma brought me to see the kid. It was a girl. Looked just like any baby to me. She was cute. I said it to me da when I got home, told him I thought she was a lovely little thing – I couldn't have been more than ten or eleven. Well, he gave me such a box across the ear! Floored me, he did. "Show no weakness!" he said. "That sickness is in your blood, and you need to stay strong to make sure it doesn't get out."'

Dale drained his glass and looked at me with bloodshot eyes. 'Seems to me he was right. The sickness got out. Poor Tammy.' He stood up and left.

Poor Dale.

34

'Why can't we do a Christmas n't'v'ty play?' Gus asked.

'Well, it's getting a little bit close to Christmas to start thinking about that,' I said. 'We wouldn't really have time to practise.'

Gus was lying on the floor among the detritus of the art area. He was in the way (I was reminded of Millie in my kitchen) and Tush and I had to step over him to get the various odds and ends we needed to finish the posters advertising our Christmas party. We were inviting all the parents and any of the local shopkeepers who were interested to join us for tea and cakes before we broke up for the holidays – the past few months had been good and we wanted to mark it in some way. Gus was in danger of getting trodden on, but he seemed so depressed I hadn't the heart to move him.

'My brudder is doin' a n't'v'ty play in his school.' He sighed dejectedly. 'He says I can't do one cos all the kids in my crèche is retards.'

'You know that isn't true, Gus,' I said. 'Nobody here is a retard.'

'I tole 'im that, but he said they was, an' that I'm a bit of a retard too. Mammy shouted at him and gave him a slap in the head, but he still said it. He din' take it back neither.'

Tush was listening carefully, her tongue stuck out from between her teeth as she glued one of the children's cardboard Christmas parcels to her poster.

'Well, maybe we can do a nativity play, Gus,' she said.

'Um . . . how are we going to manage it, Tush?' I asked.

'Yeah, tell 'im.' Gus sat up, looking much perkier all of a sudden.

'The kids put on plays almost every day, don't they?' Tush said. 'I bet they can come up with some kind of Christmas story fairly quickly. The costumes aren't a big deal. We can perform it when the parents come in.'

'That's on Friday. This is Monday,' I said.

'Great,' Tush said, smiling. 'That gives us four days to rehearse.'

Gus let out a whoop and blitzed his way around the room, shouting, 'We're doin' a n't'v'ty play! We're doin' a n't'v'ty play!'

Lonnie and Susan looked up at us, bemused. All I could do was shrug. It looked as if the decision had been made.

Tush's confidence that the children could formulate a recognizable Christmas story proved to be somewhat misplaced. Coming up with a story was no problem – they were all full of stories. The issue was that the stories tended to change significantly every time the kids acted them out, and that they usually bore no relation to Christmas or to the gospel telling of Joseph and Mary arriving in Bethlehem to find no room at the inn.

I was beginning to despair. I didn't mind the kids presenting a ramshackle drama for their parents – no one expects perfection from pre-schoolers, let alone pre-schoolers with special needs – but I thought it important that the children demonstrate at least a loose comprehension of what Christmas was about.

Gus was the most coherent member of the group. He insisted that a 'n't'v'ty' play *had* to have 'Jophus and Mary' in it, and that the baby Jesus had to put in an appearance, although the mechanics of this seemed to evade him – he had gone so far as to suggest that Lonnie might play this important figure, and come on to the stage at the end of the performance singing 'Happy Birthday to Me'.

It was Rufus's dad, Bill, who presented us with the answer to our problem. I had sent a note home with Rufus inviting Bill to pop in to see how well the tree he had donated was doing. On the Wednesday before our scheduled performance Bill arrived, looking nervous and a little embarrassed, but unable to hide his delight at how lovely his gift looked.

A mug of strong tea in hand, he paused to watch Ross as Joseph, Milandra as Mary, and Jeffrey and Tammy as shepherds, all dressed in towels and other strips of material, being fed lines by Tush.

'Is this the baby the angels told us about?' Tush hissed.

'Is dis de . . . angel . . . de baby said was . . . here . . .' the kids mumbled, looking here and there and shuffling their feet in utter disarray.

Bill shook his head in amusement. 'Y'know, when I was a lad, they used to do a nativity play in the grotto at the back of the church every year,' he said. 'Some of the local farmers would bring an ass and a goat and that. It was lovely.'

'Yeah?' I said, not really listening, wishing I had never let Tush talk us into this disaster.

'Ye should do that. You and the lads,' Bill said. 'I can get the animals off me mate Johno.'

'What?' I asked. 'Um . . . hold on a minute . . . how did it work, these plays?'

He told me, and I realized that this might just be the lifeline we needed.

It was so simple, but so beautiful.

That Friday evening, surrounded by a group of proud parents and delighted local business people, and not a small number who had come along to see a play, we created a living, breathing crib, a nativity scene with a heartbeat.

The script was provided directly from the Gospel of Luke, and we decided that Tush should read it, and the children act out what she read. The text is so rich in detail and the action so iconic it gave them plenty of work to do. So, on that crisp, frosty evening, as dusk settled, we made our way to the old church just off the village's main street. We'd had tea and a wonderful variety of food, mostly supplied by Mulligan's, in the crèche, and although the kids' artwork and various other accomplishments were on display, the only thing discussed was the play.

Bill had already set up the stage for us, cordoning off an area with bales of hay where the donkey and the goat were tethered happily. A box filled with straw did admirably for a crib. When the audience and actors were assembled Tush, looking fairly angelic herself with cheeks rosy from the cold, stepped up to the microphone the parish priest had provided, and began to read lines written two thousand years ago.

'"Now it happened in those days that a decree went out from Caesar Augustus that everyone in the world should be counted. All the people went to write their names on the list, everyone to his own city. Joseph went up from Galilee to the city of David, which is called Bethlehem, to enrol himself with Mary, because they were going to be married, and she was soon going to have a baby. It happened, while they were there, that the day came that she should give birth. She

227

brought forth her first-born son, and she wrapped him in bands of cloth, and laid him in a feeding trough, because there was no room for them in the inn."'

Each line was intoned slowly, and the children acted out their parts to perfection. When it came time for Jesus to be laid in the manger, Milandra, as Mary, produced from behind the box a doll, wrapped in cloth. I peered over to see which one it was, because the face was very definitely black. To my amazement, in the light of the candles that illuminated the scene, I realized her baby Jesus was none other than the doll Susan had given her for her birthday – still with no legs and only one arm.

I looked over at Susan. She had tears in her eyes.

Felicity and Tony stood front and centre and, despite our previous antagonism, I saw nothing but love and pride in the man's eyes. Mitzi's parents had come to see the performance, too, and there was no doubt that they had set aside any philosophical or theological issues they might have had about Christmas. When their daughter sang 'Silent Night', they could have burst with pride. The only parents, in fact, who were notably absent were Kylie and Dale. Tammy played her role as a shepherd with her usual stoicism, neither particularly enthusiastic nor doggedly disruptive. I felt awful for her – every other child had at least one parent in attendance. But if she was disappointed she never once let on, and accepted the audience's applause calmly.

We went home that night full of good cheer – and why not? Despite the fact that the performance had ended with a rendition of 'The Elephant Song', everyone decreed that it was the most authentic nativity play they'd ever seen.

35

I drove home to Wexford on Christmas Eve to spend the holidays with my family. I ate and drank far too much, watched the same old movies for the millionth time (can you *ever* truly see *Casablanca* too often?), and walked Millie along the beach at Kaat's Strand, where she charged into the foam like a thing possessed, only to lurch right back out again when she discovered how cold the water was.

I had invited Lonnie to join me, but he had turned my offer down flat – he said he had made other arrangements, though he refused to tell me what they were. I suspected they involved spending the day alone on the mountain, probably watching the same movies as me but with something peculiar he had prepared for himself to eat instead of the traditional fare. I didn't force the issue. Lonnie was entitled to his pride and dignity – he had spent enough of his life trying to preserve them.

On New Year's Eve at around ten o'clock it started to snow, and didn't stop. I sat in the living room in my father's house and watched it build up on the green in drifts of pure, unblemished white. Before long children were out in the frigid night air building snowmen and having snowball fights.

When I went to bed I left the curtains open and watched the huge, fat snowflakes drifting downwards until sleep claimed me.

I expected that we'd have snow for a day or so, after which a thaw would set in and everything would get back to normal, but Jack Frost had other ideas, and as the days crept dangerously close to the date for me to return to work, the weather didn't break. In fact, the forecast on 2 January informed us that the temperature in Wexford that night was only a couple of degrees warmer than it was at the North Pole.

The following day I called Lonnie. 'We're snowed in,' I said.

'No shit. I am actually speaking to you from an igloo. I went out for a walk, and when I came back the house was buried. I had no choice but to fashion a shelter out of ice. It was a matter of survival.'

'Can you try to be serious for just one brief moment? How bad is it up there?'

'It's pretty bad. But some of the farmers are venturing out on tractors and whatnot. One or two of the roads have been cleared.'

'Little Scamps is due to open tomorrow. Should I try and make it up to ye?'

'*Can* you make it up is a more pertinent question?'

I thought about that. 'According to the news the main roads are more or less passable. And the Austin is a really good car in snow. It's got a low centre of gravity.'

'Nice to know it's good for something. Look, if you make it, I'll go in with you. Don't have anything better to do.'

'How was Christmas?' I asked him.

'It was okay,' he said.

'Where'd you go?'

'Oh – you know – I was around.'

I sighed. 'You were on your own, weren't you?'

'Not completely.'

'Oh? Who were you with, then?'

He paused for a second, obviously deciding whether to tell me or not. 'Tush called around.'

'On Christmas Day?'

'Yeah. And on Stephen's Day. And we spent New Year's Eve together too, if you must know.' This last sentence came out in a rush, as if, now that he had started talking, he couldn't stop.

'You fucking *dog*!' I said. 'You kept that one on the down-low, didn't you?'

'Well, you know how quiet and unassuming I am,' he said. 'Introverted, some might call me.'

I laughed. 'I want to hear all about it when I see you. I'm going to try and do the drive today – in fact I'm going to leave as soon as possible, while the daylight holds.'

'All right,' Lonnie said. 'Go carefully. Call me when you get in.'

The drive was a nightmare. Ireland is known for its temperate weather (which means it rains a lot, but never usually gets very hot or particularly cold). As a result when we do get extreme weather, the entire country shuts down.

Most of the main roads had been cleared and the going was good, but I lived within a maze of tiny, winding, narrow roads that couldn't even be called secondary in a fit of dubious generosity. The Austin does go like a dream on snow and ice, but even with its dogged grip on the road surface, there were still times when I was convinced I was going to end up in a ditch or, worse still, in the back of the car in front of me.

I stopped for petrol at a forecourt somewhere in the middle of my journey. I was tired, suffering from caffeine withdrawal, and Millie needed a run around – dogs will sleep most of the time on long journeys, but there comes a time when even the laziest mutt needs some air.

I was leaning against the bonnet of my car, sipping from a Styrofoam mug of coffee while Millie snuffled around the grass verge, when a van I thought I recognized pulled in at the pumps. A young man, shaven headed and wearing an oily-looking leather jacket, got out and started to fill up with diesel. It wasn't until Kylie got out of the other door and walked past me into the shop that I realized who they were.

Kylie didn't recognize me, either, and it wasn't until I said, 'Hi,' when she was on her way back that she spotted me at all.

'Oh. Hello,' she said, clearly uneasy around me, out of her comfort zone as she was.

'Did Tammy have a good Christmas?' I asked.

'Yeah, yeah,' Kylie said, hugging herself against the cold. 'Quiet, wasn't it?'

'My family tend to be fairly noisy,' I said. 'She with you?'

'No, one of my neighbours has her. Dale had to go and see a friend,' Kylie said.

Dale had seen me too, now, and made no effort to hide a scowl. 'I'm goin' t' use the jacks,' he shouted over, and made a beeline for the toilets.

We were quiet for a few moments, uncomfortable in each other's company.

Finally I said, 'Tammy is an amazing little girl.'

'Do you think?' Kylie asked.

'I do. She never ceases to surprise me. I think she's an incredible kid.'

Kylie didn't seem to know what to do with that. 'Do you have kids?' she asked.

'No,' I said. 'Haven't been blessed with them yet.'

She nodded, as if that explained a lot. 'If you did, maybe it'd change your mind about certain things.'

I sipped my coffee and said nothing. Millie had ranged a little bit beyond what I considered a comfortable distance, and I whistled for her to come back. She ignored me for a second – she was chewing something she probably shouldn't – then started to make her way slowly towards the car.

'Havin' kids is tough, y'know. Dunno how me 'n' Dale've stayed together through it all.'

'You're lucky to have a relationship like that,' I said.

'We're a team, so we are.' She paused. 'Sometimes I think havin' Tammy made us stronger. Other times I think she tore a huge chunk outta me heart.'

'Kids'll do that,' I said.

'I wanted to have an abortion,' Kylie said. 'Just fuckin' get rid of the thing.'

The thing, I thought. This is Tammy she's talking about.

'But Dale wouldn't hear of it,' she continued.

'Good for him,' I said. 'Lot of men wouldn't give a damn.'

Dale came out of the toilet block and started to walk in our direction. Kylie glanced at him and shuddered, as if waking from a deep sleep. 'I'll see you,' she said, and got back into the van.

I let Millie get a little more air, then followed suit.

The entire trip usually took three hours and lasted six. I was exhausted and very grumpy by the time I finally unlocked the door to my cottage, muttering obscenities about having to stand in the cold while Millie scouted about for somewhere suitable to relieve herself. I texted Lonnie to let him know we had landed safely, then lit the fire and made a hot whiskey. With *Rio Bravo* on TV and my dog snuggled up beside me on the couch, life seemed a lot friendlier. And I only wanted a cigarette a little.

I left early the next morning to pick up Lonnie, assuming that the mountain road would be treacherous, but in fact it was fairly clear – the farmers who used it on the way to tend their sheep must have made a point of keeping it gritted.

'Happy new year,' my friend said, as he hopped in.

'Back at you,' I said. 'You need any wood or coal or anything? We can pick some up on the way home.'

'No. I went into the village with Tush yesterday and we stocked up.'

I glanced at him out of the corner of my eye, but his face was obscured by the enormous fur-lined hood of his coat, and I couldn't see if he was grinning.

'Lonnie, you're going to have to tell me what happened.'

'No, I am not,' he said, and I was sure I heard a laugh in his voice.

'You owe me that much. Come on – I invited you to my father's place for Christmas. Who else is going to inflict you on their family? Huh? Is that not worth something?'

'All right, all right,' he said, and he was definitely laughing. 'She called over on Christmas Eve. We . . . um . . . talked.'

'Talked?'

'Yeah. You know – about our relationship. And stuff.'

'And did you decide anything?'

'Well . . .' Lonnie paused. How much did he feel comfortable telling me? 'I will say that Tush and I are together.'

'What does that mean?' I asked, more out of devilment than anything else.

'It means that we're going out as boyfriend and girlfriend, all right?'

'I see. And are you both ... you know ... I mean, did you ...'

'A gentleman does not kiss and tell,' he said.

'I see,' I said, enjoying winding him up. 'You know what that means, of course, don't you?'

'What?'

'It means that you have something *to* tell.'

'Listen, this conversation is over,' Lonnie said, crossing his arms with great finality.

I drove on for half a mile, neither of us speaking. Finally I said, 'Lonnie?'

'What?' he barked.

'Congratulations, man.'

'Thanks,' he said, and the smile was unmistakable in his voice this time.

36

The community centre where Little Scamps was based was like an ice block when we arrived, so Lonnie and I busied ourselves about the building, getting the heating going, putting something warming on the stove for breakfast and making the place as pleasant as possible. I had no idea how many children would arrive, but we had a responsibility to be open: many of our parents would have jobs that required them to work regardless of unpleasant weather conditions.

As it happened, only Gus and Tammy showed up. We had a high-spirited breakfast of porridge, buttered toast and hot chocolate, and Gus regaled us with stories of his Christmas bounty. Tammy, as usual, was silent throughout, but seemed to enjoy herself. Gus had arrived loaded with toys, but Tammy was characteristically empty handed.

'Did Santa come to see you, Tam?' I asked, as she sat beside me at the table, her legs dangling.

She nodded.

'Want to tell me what you got?' I enquired hopefully.

She shook her head and returned to her bowl of porridge. There was no point in pushing things any further.

Neither was there any point in putting much of a shape on the day. With just two children in our group, Lonnie and I initiated a fairly easy routine, consisting mostly of free play. At around eleven thirty Gus asked if he and Tammy might hear about Samuel Whiskers and Tom Kitten again and I happily obliged. We sang some songs and then had lunch, and in the early afternoon we did some arts and crafts.

Lonnie could do amazing things with paper. His long, deft fingers would twist and fold a small sheet into a bird, a stag, a fox or a butterfly in just one or two rapid movements. Tammy, of all the children, loved this. She would gaze at him, eyes wide, as he placed each new creation in a little line, as if all the animals were going on parade just for her.

He was doing this during the afternoon's art session, and I was on the other side of the table trying to make either head or tail of a letter that had arrived that morning from the HSE. It was written in the kind of official language only an organization as befuddled and autocratic as the health services can use and believe is effective.

'They seem to be saying there are new guidelines for the running of early-years services coming on stream, but in the same sentence they're telling me we don't have to observe them if we don't want to,' I said, feeling a headache coming on.

'Want me to turn the letter into a snowflake?' Lonnie asked.

'G – U – S! That spells "Gus"!' Gus said.

He had a sheet of white paper in front of him, and a blue crayon in his hand. He was writing his name in big, confident capitals again and again on the page.

'Hey, that's great, Gus,' I said. 'You learned to write your name in capital letters over the holiday.'

'No, I din't,' Gus said. 'See dis crayon?'

'Yeah?'

'Dis is my *magic* crayon,' he said. ''Member? I showed you afore.'

I did remember, but it had been so long ago it had never occurred to me that he would still have it. It was about half the size it had been when last he had declared its mystical properties, and looked as if it had spent some time under a bed or couch – a lot of fluff and dust was stuck to it – and a person or dog had chewed one end and left toothmarks. Gus seemed not one bit concerned about its sorry appearance.

'Wit dis magic crayon, I can write my name any time I wants to. See: G – U – S – that spells "Gus"! I writed that.'

Tammy was watching him. Lonnie was deep in concentration, fashioning another paper member of his menagerie.

'That is a really, really cool crayon, Augustus,' I said. 'Can you write anything else?'

'Just axe me. Just axe me to write anything, and I bet I can do it.'

I thought about his challenge. 'Can you write the letter . . . A?'

Gus ruffled his hair and puffed out his cheeks as if this was a huge request. 'I dunno,' he said. '"A" is one of the hardest letters to write. Everyone knows that.'

'Do you think the crayon can manage it?'

'Well, we better see. Here I go. The letter "A".'

He drew a slightly wobbly, but quite legible representation of the letter on his page, sitting back as if exhausted by the effort. 'There – I done it. It wadn' easy, let me tell ya.'

I clapped. 'Well done, Gus,' I said. 'That's some crayon you've got there.'

'It's very magic, you know.'

'Is it?'

'Yeah. It is. I think it used to be the crayon of a wizard or something.'

I nodded. 'That's probably it.'

'I have the power now.'

'You sure do.'

Something occurred to me. 'Do you think,' I asked Gus, 'that crayon might work for someone else?'

'It might,' he said, not sure at all.

'I mean, if you were to loan it to Tammy for a second, d'you reckon she might be able to write her name – or anything else?'

Gus pondered that. He looked at the grubby crayon. Tossed it up and down on the palm of his hand. Wiped his nose on his sleeve. 'Tell ya what,' he said at last. 'We'll give it a try. I can't *promise* my crayon will work for everyone, but maybe if we thinks really hard about it, it might.'

Gus handed me the crayon and I reached over and put it in front of Tammy. She looked at it as if it might give her a nasty infection. 'Why don't you see if you can use the magic?' I asked. 'I bet it'll work for you.' I pushed a sheet of paper across the table so it was within easy reach. Tammy curled her lip, then reached her tiny hand and dragged the paper to her. Giving me a really evil look, she picked up the blue wax crayon.

'Could you write your name, Tammy?' I asked.

Tammy looked at the page and scratched at it for a few seconds.

'She *is* writin' her name,' Gus said in wonder. 'The magic *is* workin'.'

After only a second or two, Tammy stopped and rolled the crayon back across the table. Then she hopped off her chair and went to her haven in the book corner.

'Did you write your name, Tam?' I asked, getting up and walking around to where she had been sitting.

There, in big blue letters, was a single word: 'NO.'

'Think she's trying to tell you something?' Lonnie asked, as he set a paper crane down at the end of his line.

37

When the thaw came it settled in slowly. The roads were clear by the third week in January, but there were still chunks of grimy grey snow clumped by the verges. Tiny particles of ice danced in the air in the early mornings where dew had frozen as it fell earthwards.

All the children came back to Little Scamps and life returned to some semblance of normality – well, almost normal.

The main change was in Milandra. I had expected her to come back in a raging fury, having unlearned everything we had gone to such lengths to teach her before Christmas. This, however, did not occur. In fact she was, if anything, even better behaved: more thoughtful, gentler and generally much more pleasant to be around.

She offered to help Gilbert get his coat on at home-time, wanted to set out the plates and jam-jars at breakfast, and was the first to share toys and books. We still had outbursts – she hadn't turned into a saint – but the overall effect was quite surprising.

'Do you think we're dealing with an "invasion of the bodysnatchers" type of thing?' Susan asked, as we watched Milandra helping Mitzi – over Christmas she'd put back maybe three-quarters of the weight she'd lost – on to her chair.

'I did wonder,' I said. 'But I'm actually just glad. That little girl should be in school. I'm going to ask Tristan to find out if we can't get her assessed by an educational psychologist, see if the local primary school might take her next September.'

'Have you talked to her parents about it?'

I sighed.

'No. But I will. I reckon it might not be a bad thing to have Tammy there checked out, too. I believe that child is hiding an awful lot.'

I did the bus run that evening and spoke to Felicity (Tony, thankfully, was nowhere to be seen), who was delighted for Milandra to be assessed if we could arrange it. When I arrived at Tammy's house I found Dale, her dad, in the garden, bundled up in a parka and woollen hat, an old racing bicycle turned upside down on the path. Tammy stood back, as if she was waiting to see what might happen.

'Dale,' I said, holding out my gloved hand. 'Good to see you again.'

He nodded and continued trying to get the rusty chain back on to its mechanism.

'How's the car runnin'?' he asked, then: 'Go on in the house, Tamarra.'

The child went in through the open front door.

'Yeah, it's doing great,' I said, smiling. 'Haven't had any trouble with it since. But listen, I'm here to ask you something.'

'What?'

'Dale, I believe that Tammy is gifted and I want to have her assessed by a psychologist. I'd like to have your permission to do so.'

The man swore and rattled about in a tool-box for a different wrench. 'Is it going to cost me anything?' he asked.

'No,' I said.

'Then do what you fucking like,' he said.

It was obvious there was to be no more discussion. I went back to the bus.

When I called Tristan about setting up the assessments, he told me there was a waiting list of at least twelve months. I pointed out that we did not have that long – while there was no great rush for Tammy, who was only three, Milandra would have to take up her place in eight months, and would need time to prepare for such a monumental move.

'It's always a pressure cooker with you, isn't it?' He sighed.

'Things change fast around here,' I said. 'You've got to be able to roll with the punches.'

'I'll see what I can do,' he said. 'I might be able to call in some favours.'

A week later I had a call from Helena McQueen, a psychologist from the National Educational Psychological Services.

The assessment for Milandra was really just a formality. Helena, a bookish, quietly spoken woman in her early forties, spent an hour or so observing her at play with the other children, then took her into the office and did a series of IQ tests, looking at her capacity to understand numbers, words and some other concepts she would need to function within a classroom setting. She also looked at some of the work Milandra had done at Little Scamps – her art, some of the notes she had placed in the KB, and listened to us describing the changes we had seen in her over the time she had been with us.

'Usually I would go away and consider the evidence,' Helena said, 'but there is absolutely no doubt in my mind that Milandra is quite ready for school. In fact, I would strongly recommend she go directly into senior infants, with children of her own age group.'

'Skip a year?' Tush said. 'Wouldn't that overwhelm her?'

'I don't think she'll notice,' Helena said. 'She'll be starting in a new place, anyway, and she's more than ready for the academics.'

Tammy was a more difficult proposition. She was hugely suspicious of Helena, and initially refused to acknowledge her presence. But the psychologist was well used to unco-operative children, and won her over within an hour or two of dogged perseverance (and some white chocolate buttons – never underestimate the power of bribery).

I had no idea how she was going to assess a child who was determinedly non-verbal, but Helena assured me it was quite possible. 'There are many tests that require neither words nor the capacity to use sign language. I can already tell from observing Tammy and communicating with her that she has at least a normal grasp of language for her age. Leave her with me and we'll see what else we can learn.'

Helena and Tammy went off into the office together, and I could see them through the glass, both obviously deep in concentration. An hour later they emerged, and Tammy ran off to join her friends, who were playing skittles in the entrance hallway, which, long and thin, was perfect for the game.

'That is a very bright child,' Helena said, unable to hide a smile. 'I would say she's operating at a good three or four years beyond her age range, and I haven't even been able to assess her verbal reasoning properly. I can tell you this, though – she can read, and read well.'

'We suspected as much,' I said, 'but she's always blocked any attempt we made to prove it.'

'One of the ways we test non-verbal children is to give

them visual problems to solve,' Helena explained. 'We do things like showing them a series of shapes, all different colours, and ask them to pick out the red circle. Or we show them a picture of a field of sheep with one cow in it, and ask them to choose the odd one out. That sort of thing.'

'I would imagine she sailed through it,' I said.

'She did. So I went up a notch. She's, what, three?'

'She'll be four in a month and a half.'

'Children of her age should be just about able to put things in sequence along one set of characteristics. So, if I ask her to put all the red blocks in a row out of a pile, she should be able to do it, but I would expect her to have trouble with all the *triangular* red bricks. Not Tammy. I tried a different sort of sequencing test. I showed her a series of cards with the days of the week written on them. Except they were running the wrong way around. Instead of Monday, Tuesday, Wednesday and so on, these went Sunday, Saturday, Friday.'

'So you showed her a series of *words*?' I said.

'The trick to solving series problems is working out the rule,' Helena said. 'But with this one, she had to be able to read the words to be able to work it out. But she did. Paused for all of ten seconds before arranging them into the correct order.'

I wanted to leap about like Tom Cruise on *The Oprah Winfrey Show*, but held back.

'The days of the week are on every calendar in every room in the world,' I said. 'Look, we have them on the timetable over there. Isn't it possible she saw them as *shapes*, symbols she recognized, and had memorized the order?'

Helena grinned. 'I gather you've studied child psychology.'

'Little bit. But, really, isn't that possible?'

'It is, but I'm a little more thorough than that. I then showed her the words "red", "blue", "yellow", "black" and "sweet", and asked her which was the odd one out. She chose "sweet" without hesitation.'

I sat back, suddenly a little light headed. 'Shit,' I said.

'My thoughts exactly,' Helena said. 'You have a gifted child on your hands.'

38

The four staff from Little Scamps sat opposite Tony and Felicity, Milandra's parents. We had asked Dale and Kylie, Tammy's mother and father, to come to the meeting as well but they hadn't arrived. I didn't think it was likely they would at this stage, so we began.

It was clear within three minutes that this was not going to be an easy process. Rather than being delighted at his daughter's progress and excited about her making the transition into primary school, Tony was furious. Felicity sat beside him, pale and teary eyed, saying little.

'I do not know how you could do this without my permission,' he said, his voice raised and his eyes wide.

'Well, I did ask your wife,' I said. 'And it's not as if we were putting Milandra forward for invasive surgery –. the tests she undertook were quite normal for a child in her circumstances.'

'Really? And what, precisely, are her *circumstances*?'

'She is a child in a special facility for children with physical, intellectual and behavioural problems, mostly within the mild range,' Lonnie said, intoning the definition deadpan, as if he was reading it from a textbook.

'Is that why you're here, little man?' Tony asked, leering at Lonnie.

I saw Tush twitch at the insult.

'No,' Lonnie said. 'I'm here because of my charm and good looks.'

'This is ridiculous,' I said. 'I know you've been posted the report from the educational psychologist. You've seen the results of the psychometric testing. I cannot understand why you're so upset. This is *good* news, for God's sake.'

'I do not need you, or anyone else, to tell me how clever my daughter is,' Tony said.

'So you don't believe us?' Susan said. 'Is that it? Would you like to have her tested yourselves? I can assure you that the results will be exactly the same.'

'You have destroyed her,' Tony spat.

'What?' the four of us said, almost in chorus.

'You heard me,' he said. 'She has no fire any more. No fierceness. How is she supposed to survive?'

'Good Lord,' I said. 'That's what this is all about? She's not mad enough for you any more?'

Tony stormed out, leaving Felicity where she was, tears streaming down her cheeks.

'You're going to have to help us understand what we've done wrong,' Susan said to her, 'because I'm at a loss.'

Felicity nodded and took a tissue out of her handbag, which looked as if it had cost more than the building we were sitting in. 'It's hard to explain,' she said, wiping her eyes.

'Try,' Susan said. 'You might be surprised at how smart we are.'

And Felicity talked. She talked for more than an hour. And when she was finished, we did understand – sort of. Our understanding was pretty unimportant, though, because the

247

only really important thing was that, without Tony's say-so, Milandra would be unable to go anywhere.

Tony didn't come back – I don't know where he went, but when we walked his wife out to the car, she drove off alone.

The salt marsh looked a bitter, lonely place in the winter's night. The moon was only occasionally visible when the clouds broke, and a vicious, cutting wind was blowing in from the sea. I could hear waves crashing against the coast, and there was the smell of salt spray in the air. Through the thin wooden door I could hear a television, but nothing else. I knocked, and was surprised when the door was answered.

'Hey, Kylie,' I said. 'Sorry to call so late, but I'd like to talk to you about Tammy.'

I couldn't smell any alcohol off the woman, but she still appeared to be a bit out of it.

'Yeah,' she said, scrunching her eyes up as if she was concentrating hard. 'Tammy. Yeah, okay. You'd best come in, then.'

'Thank you.'

The living room was lit by the television screen. Dale was sitting in front of it – nearly on top of it, actually. Tammy was sitting on the floor, a magazine open in front of her.

'Hi, Dale,' I said. 'How are you, Tammy?'

Dale nodded, but didn't look pleased to see me. Neither did Tammy, for that matter. Kylie sat on the couch opposite, the arm of which I settled my behind on.

'Did you receive a letter from the Health Board about those tests we ran on Tammy?' I asked.

It was as if I was speaking to three non-verbal individuals. The only sound that met my question came from the television.

'It's kind of important that you read it,' I said, keeping my voice level and my tone friendly. 'It tells us a lot of things we didn't know – or at least weren't sure of – about Tammy.'

Dale swore explosively and aggressively, then muted the television using an ancient remote control that had been taped up to stop it falling apart. 'Would you make your fucking point, buddy?' he barked. 'I'm tryin' to watch this, and you are gettin' on me nerves, right?'

Tammy was sitting very still and blinked at the outburst, but otherwise seemed unmoved by it.

'Did you know your daughter could read?' I asked.

'Don't be fuckin' stupid,' Dale said scornfully. 'She's only a baby.'

'She reads very well, at a level far above what would usually be expected for her age,' I said. 'She also has an excellent grasp of numbers and can understand abstract concepts kids far older than her would struggle with. She's not just bright, Dale, she's gifted.'

Dale looked at his daughter, who was staring at us with an unreadable expression, then back at me. 'I think you're pullin' my leg,' he said. 'That young one's a dope. Anyone could tell you that. She's been strange since she was a baby. She's never done nothin' kids're meant to. Shit, she don't even talk. Now you're comin' in here all high and fuckin' mighty and tellin' me she's some sort of genius? Get the fuck outta here, man. Not my kid.'

'Why does it scare you to have a gifted child?' I asked. 'You should be proud.'

'Maybe we should listen to him,' Kylie said. 'I always thought Tamarra was smart.'

'Shut up, you,' Dale snapped. 'You're stoned out of your tree. You don't even know what he's talkin' about.'

'I always thought you were brainy, Tamster,' Kylie said. 'I knew you were special.'

'She's special all right,' Dale said. 'Special in the head.'

'Don't insult her, please,' I said. I'd about had enough. I had delivered good news to two sets of parents, and received nothing in return but grief. I knew childcare could be a thankless task, but this was ridiculous. And I was not going to sit there while he made fun of Tammy.

'It's none o' your business what I do with me own,' Dale said.

'Maybe not,' I said. 'But that doesn't mean I can't have an opinion.'

Dale considered that one. He didn't know whether or not I was making fun of him. He decided it didn't matter. 'Fuck it,' he said. 'You're only a babysitter anyway. Paid to wipe kids' arses and keep 'em out o' trouble. And you can't even do that!'

'I am proud of what I do,' I said. 'Your daughter is an amazing little girl. It just sickens me that you don't see it. You spend so much of your time getting wasted you haven't even taken the time to get to know her.'

'You can't tell me what to do, you uppity fucker,' Dale snarled. 'You aren't a social worker. You have no power over me or my kid.'

'No,' I said. 'Not today.'

I stood. This was going nowhere. It was possibly even making things worse in the long run. 'Would you at least think about this?' I said, trying one last time. 'Tammy is going to have to leave Little Scamps eventually. When she does, she is going to need a placement that will nurture her abilities. Lonnie, Su, Tush or I can work with you on finding somewhere suitable, and we can help you to raise the money – most schools that cater for gifted children have a scholarship programme. What do you think, Tam?'

I suddenly realized she was gone. Turning, I saw that the front door was ajar. 'I think she's run off,' I said.

'She'll be back,' Dale drawled.

'Where would she have gone?' I asked. 'It's freezing out.'

'She has hidin' places out on the marsh,' Kylie said. 'You'll never find her.'

'She wouldn't go out there at this time of night, would she?' I asked. 'I mean, it's miserable.'

Both parents shrugged.

'I'm going to bring her back,' I said.

I went to the door, pulling my collar up and wrapping my scarf closer about me. I was more than a little angry with Kylie and Dale. *No*, I thought. *I am not a social worker – but I know plenty, and a visit could so easily be arranged.* I put such thoughts out of my mind and trotted across the road to the low wall that divided the estate from the adjoining scrubland. The darkness had that muddy, murky quality it can acquire when the air is heavy with rain or mist. I decided I had better be sensible and jogged back to the car, where I took a small torch from the glove compartment – I keep it there in case of a puncture on a dark night – then climbed into the wilderness. I was about to set off when I heard a call.

'Hey – wait up there.'

It was Dale, dressed in a ludicrously flimsy jacket.

'Not havin' you sayin' I don't look after me own.'

'Glad to have you along,' I said truthfully. I took a step.

'Better warn you – watch your step. This place is full of sink holes.'

'Full of what?'

'The ground gets soft all sudden like. You're walkin' along grand and then you're up to your neck in muck – just like that. It's like . . . um . . . quicksand.'

'And you let Tammy play here?'

'*Let* ain't got nothin' t' do with it,' Dale said, and set off into the swamp.

I switched on the torch and concentrated its beam ahead of us. Out on the flats the wind was so high that talking was futile. Seeing wasn't easy, either. With every strong gust of wind we were slapped with a ferocious squall of rain and hail. Within moments Dale was soaked to the skin and shivering. My coat held out a little better, but I knew it was only a matter of time before I was in the same condition.

I was deeply concerned about navigation. I thought I could hear the sea to my right, but the environment through which we were gingerly trudging was so monotonous it was impossible to make out any distinct landmarks. The only things rising above the spongy ground were desolate whin bushes and twisted, gnarled trees. If Tammy had found a place to shelter, I couldn't for the life of me see it.

Since moving to the country, I had taken to wearing walking boots as my usual footwear. They are ideal for trekking across mountains and heaths, but the marsh highlighted their major flaw: while they are waterproof, they are no good at all if you step in a puddle deeper than your ankle – the water just flows in over the top of the boot and floods it. Within five minutes I might as well have been sloshing along with my feet in two buckets of ice water.

We'd been walking for around a quarter of an hour and I could no longer see the lights of the houses in the little estate. I tugged at Dale's sleeve. 'Do you know where we're going?' I shouted over the gale.

'There!' he said, pointing at what looked like a smudge of grey on the horizon.

It was some kind of subterranean storage shed, built low to the ground with the actual room dug into the earth.

'She hides out in there, sometimes,' Dale said.

I got down on my knees, feeling the damp seeping through the legs of my jeans, and shone the torch into the cellar, illuminating a wide space lined with moss-speckled breeze blocks. I was just in time to see two little legs disappear through a space in the opposite wall.

'She's gone out the other side,' I shouted, and we both took off after the child, whose shape I could just pick up in the torchlight as she headed even deeper into the marsh, desperate in her attempt to get away from us.

It was like being trapped in some kind of waking nightmare from which there was no escape. The ground was rough and unstable – on one occasion I went up to my knee in a hole and Dale had to haul me out. I tried to keep Tammy in our sights, but she seemed to know the area far better than we did, and hopped from tussock to tussock with amazing agility. I seemed to lose her for long minutes at a time, then catch sight of her again.

'Where the hell is she leading us?' I shouted.

'Fucked if I know,' he said. 'Never been this far in.'

'Tammy,' I called. 'Come on back, baby. Your dad and I are friends now!'

I glimpsed her blond tresses and then she was gone again. I ran onwards.

This time we couldn't find her again. It felt as if we were very near the coast. I was certain I could hear the regular smash of waves, like a heartbeat, and the taste of salt on my tongue was very strong. I was running across sand, now, and I could see shells among the detritus and reeds.

'Tammy!' I called again.

'Tammy!' Dale called, too. There was panic in his voice, and I knew it was real.

In her terror, the child had led us far, far from home, and this was not a safe place.

We were standing on the edge of an inlet now. The water washed in in freezing sheets, rimmed with yellow foam. I ran the beam of the torch around the edge, and thought I saw a patch of something a different shade from the rest. I flicked the light back and, lo and behold, there was Tammy. She was holding on to some reeds on the shore for dear life – the rest of her was stuck in the mud – only her chest and shoulders could be seen above it.

'Hold still, Tam,' I shouted. 'We're coming!'

Tammy saw us and waved one hand. 'Help me!' she called. 'Help me!'

Her voice was hoarse from lack of use – and fear.

'Did she just talk?' Dale panted.

'She did,' I said.

Then we were beside her, and she was on safe, solid ground and we were all sobbing, lying in the dirt on a stormy night, far from anywhere.

'I don' wanna leave L'il Scamps,' Tammy sobbed. 'Don' make me go, Shane.'

'Honey, you're too little to go anywhere,' I said, laughing and crying all at the same time. 'You have a lot of time ahead of you in Little Scamps, and you'll be more than ready before you have to leave us. You got all confused.'

'I don't have to go?' she asked.

'No,' I said. 'You don't.'

'I can stay in the crèche, Daddy?'

'You sure can,' Dale said. 'When you're big enough, we'll talk about a school for you. Shane here says you're real smart, and we gotta get the right place for you.'

''Kay,' Tammy said.

Dale carried her home. He was exhausted, but I knew better than to offer to take a turn with her. He needed to shoulder the burden of his daughter. I wasn't going to deprive him of that privilege.

39

Lonnie and I were walking Millie on the mountain near his house. It was a beautiful crisp, cold afternoon. I had allowed him to talk me into having dinner at his place, which meant enduring the horrors of his cooking. But I was feeling magnanimous, and figured I could always get take-out on the way home if things were really dire.

We followed the slope of a hill up to one of our favourite places, a peak upon which a small stone circle had been erected some time in prehistory and from where the surrounding countryside could be seen in all directions.

'Who would have thought Tammy would be such a chatterbox?' Lonnie said. 'It's been kind of hard to get a word in around Little Scamps the past few weeks.'

'She's making up for lost time, I suppose.' I laughed.

'That's for sure.' Lonnie leaned his back on a stone pillar. 'Do you think her dad's going to step up to the mark, now?' he asked. 'Be the kind of father she needs?'

I put my hands into my pockets against the cold. 'I hope so. They both had a terrible fright when they realized how close they'd come to losing one another. It brought each of them out of their shells. Tammy started talking, Dale started caring. It won't be easy for either of them – they've learned not to trust, not to value, one another. They have a hell of a lot of unlearning to do. But I think they might make it.'

I looked east, towards the sea and the location of Tammy's rebirth. It was a peculiar memory, that night – beautiful and terrifying at the same time.

'There's something I want to talk to you about, mate,' I said.

'Out with it,' he said.

'How would you like to take over managing Little Scamps?'

He chuckled drily. 'And where are you going?'

'It was only ever supposed to be temporary,' I said. 'I've loved my time with the kids, but I don't see myself working in early years for the rest of my life. And there's no use saying I'll wait until this group moves on – they're too wide a spread of ages. There will always be other kids coming on stream. I think the time is right. Things are running really nicely.'

In fact, I didn't want to leave. I loved the children, I had come to cherish the staff as friends, and I thought I was learning to become a good crèche worker. But I knew my departure would give Lonnie the chance he needed to flourish. He would never truly spread his wings while he was in my shadow – I was the last of the people who had stuck him on a slide to examine him like some sort of bug. If he was ever to shrug off his past, I had to go. Little Scamps was wonderful, but it was an opportunity he needed much more than I did.

'Why ask me?' Lonnie wondered. 'Why not Su or Tush?'

'They didn't want it when I arrived. They don't want it now. Anyway, you have a natural flair for the work. This is your area, Lonnie. You're really, really good at it. Little Scamps is where you're meant to be, I think.'

He watched Millie stalking a pheasant that had just come

out of the brush. The bird watched her crawling along the ground, biding its time until she was nearly upon it, then exploded into the air in a flurry of copper-coloured feathers.

'Tush and I are thinking of moving in together,' Lonnie said.

'Wow. Big step.'

'I met her parents the other day.'

'How'd that go?'

'They were . . . polite.'

'Oh. Not good, then?'

'They didn't run screaming,' he said. 'It was sort of funny hearing them trying to find other ways of saying "little" or "small". You'd be amazed how often those words crop up in an average evening.'

'I'm sorry it didn't go better,' I said.

'They might become accustomed to it,' Lonnie said.

'They might.'

'Probably not,' he said. 'I expect they think I'm some kind of phase she's going through, and that she'll grow out of me.'

'Tush is a fairly down-to-earth sort,' I said. 'The fact that she's even considering moving in with you is testament to the fact you are *not* a phase.'

'I thought that,' he said. 'But I was a little bit afraid to say it.'

We wandered towards the band of trees on the other side of a fire break.

'I don't know if we'll make it or not,' he said.

'You'll have fun trying, though,' I said. 'And if you get your heart broken, well, that's no worse than anyone else has to put up with when a relationship falls asunder.'

'But if I don't . . .' he said.

'If you don't,' I said, 'you get the best thing in the world.'

We followed the treeline until it joined a narrow path that would bring us back to Lonnie's small house.

'I found out what happened to Angelica,' Lonnie said.

'Really? How'd you do that?'

'Sister Helen, the nun who works with Tristan sometimes, she helped me. It actually wasn't difficult. Don't know why I didn't do it before.'

'Maybe you're feeling a little bit more confident in matters of the . . . er . . . heart,' I suggested.

'She went back to Poland soon after I left the school,' Lonnie said. 'She died about five years later. They think it might have been linked to the malaria. She did have it and never fully recovered from it, you see. Poor thing.'

'How do you feel, knowing that?' I asked.

'I don't know. I talked to Tush about it.'

'Good,' I said.

There didn't seem to be much more to say than that.

And two men and their dog followed the woodland path back to an unimaginative, though actually quite tasty, dinner of Cumberland sausage and roasted Brussels sprouts.

40

Tony came to see me shortly before I left Little Scamps to return to work at Drumlin. He was waiting outside the building as I locked up, looking remarkably unkempt for a man who was usually so dapper.

'Tony, if you're here to have another shouting match, I'm not interested,' I said.

'I would just like to talk,' he said. 'I do not want to fight with you.'

'Okay,' I said. 'Let's go get a cup of coffee.'

Kate's café was a short walk away, and we sat by the window.

'What can I do for you, Tony?' I asked.

'Felicity has left me,' he said. 'Or, more accurately, she threw me out.'

I sipped my coffee – Kate, as well as giving nice hugs, made a mean cup. 'I'm sorry to hear that,' I said.

'You didn't know?'

'I did not. Felicity doesn't exactly volunteer information, and Milandra has made no reference to it. She seems as happy and relaxed as she has been of late.'

Kate bustled over to see if we were okay. 'Can I get you anything else, gentlemen?'

'I'd love a slice of carrot cake,' I said.

'And you, sir?'

Tony shook his head and Kate went to get my cake.

'What is it with you people and vegetables in cakes?'

I just smiled. I'd had the reaction I was after. 'You still haven't told me what you want,' I said.

'I want you to make sure Milandra starts school in September.'

'You know I'm leaving Little Scamps,' I said.

'Yes. But you can see to it before you go.'

I nodded. 'I can do that. Why the change of heart?'

Tony looked utterly dejected. It was hard for me to feel sorry for him. I could see no reason why he had behaved so badly towards me. As far as I was concerned, he was in a situation of his own making.

When he didn't answer, I said, 'I looked up the meaning of *ôkùnrin ábökùnrinlò*.'

Tony gazed at me dolefully.

'It means "homosexual",' I continued. 'Tony, for such a smart man, you aren't very original. I've had idiots calling me that since I started working with kids. It's a lousy word to use as an insult, anyway – first of all, if I *were* gay it wouldn't bother me in the slightest, and if I weren't, you must know that someone in my line of work will have encountered people of all persuasions and had no problem with them. You're going to have to do better than that if you want to get to me.'

He didn't say anything for what seemed like an age. Then: 'Milandra seems happy.'

Kate brought my cake. Despite Milandra and Arga's reviews, it was very good.

'Your daughter *is* happy,' I said. 'She's clever, sensitive, warm and content. She is a valued member of the crèche, and of this village. You should be very proud of her.'

'I am,' he said.

I had some more cake. It had cinnamon in it. I like cinnamon. 'It took me and my friends quite a long time to get her to a place where she could function alongside other people,' I said. 'I think some good work was done at home with her, too. I don't know how much of that success is down to you. I suspect not too much. I think your lovely wife was instrumental, though.'

'I want to explain something to you,' Tony said, leaning in close.

He had bags under his eyes, the look of a man who had lost a lot of weight quickly, weight he could not afford to lose.

'I'm listening,' I said.

'You do not understand what it is like to grow up in poverty.'

I thought I might be able to mount a pretty good argument to that statement, but decided to keep my mouth shut for a bit.

'Where I come from a child has to fight,' Tony said, 'fight for every single morsel of food, every article of clothing. Every accomplishment is hard won. When I was six years old, I saw a friend of mine, a boy who was only ten, killed for his shoes. His murderer was barely twelve.'

There was other chatter going on in the café, but I couldn't hear it any more. It was just me and Tony.

'I am here, talking to you, because my parents taught me to be fierce. To never give in, to trust nobody but myself. Those skills have stood me in good stead my whole life. If I did not have them, I would be dead.'

I nodded. Felicity had explained as much that evening back at the crèche.

'I swore to myself long ago that, if I ever had a child, I

261

would teach him or her those skills too, so that if they ever found themselves in such dire need, they would be able to fight, as I did.'

'But did you not also swear that your children would never *be* in those circumstances?' I asked. 'You worked hard to rise above the awful place you grew up. You educated yourself, got a job and clawed your way to the top. You were lucky enough to marry an Irish girl whose family is well off, and you are now a man of means. Even if you lost your job in the morning, if by some ill fortune you had to sell your house and get a smaller one, if you ended up on social welfare – if all of that happened, Tony, and it would be terrible, you will *never* be destitute again. Milandra will never have to live rough or fight for scraps with other street children.'

His eyes were huge. 'I love my daughter,' he said.

'I know you do.'

'I have wronged her.'

'You made a mistake,' I said. 'It's not too late to fix it.'

He looked out of the window at the village street. Spring was coming in. It was still bright. 'You should not leave Little Scamps,' he said.

'I have another job,' I said. 'I was on loan.'

He stood. 'I am going to try and persuade my wife to have me back,' he said.

I held out my hand, and he shook it this time. 'Good luck,' I said.

'What will you do?' he asked.

'I think I might have another cup of coffee,' I said.

I watched him walk across the road to where his car was parked, then pull out into the narrow road and drive away. I knew I should go home, but it was warm and friendly in Kate's. The cook laughed behind the long counter, and a waitress smiled and winked at me as she went past. I suddenly felt very alone. Lonnie and Tush would be sitting around the little table in his kitchen, by then, probably having an early-evening drink. I didn't feel like going home to sit in an empty house.

I finished my second cup of coffee and went to my old Austin, got in and drove until the dull reverberations of the road numbed me, and I went home to my dog.

Afterword

I came to early-years work – with pre-school-aged children in crèches and playschools – with a lot of prejudice. Like many people, I was guilty of associating the hugely important work carried out in our childcare facilities with babysitting, and failed to recognize the wealth of knowledge and research done by committed and courageous staff in such settings. Much of this knowledge forms the basis of the academic texts I had studied while training to be a child-protection worker. I now understand just how vital a part of the social-care pantheon early-years work is, and am proud to have been a part of it.

The Girl Who Couldn't Smile does not feature any sexual or physical abuse. None of the parents I describe in its pages are really bad people – they are often doing their best with the hand Fate has dealt them, trying to cope with the legacy of their own childhoods. They are not wilfully neglectful of their children – they usually don't know any better.

The types of stories I recount here are, in reality, the sort most crèche workers deal with on a daily basis. The things the children say, the games they play, the activities they engage in are characteristic of those carried out in crèches and pre-schools all over Ireland, the UK and further afield.

For instance, we really did make that giant map of the village, and the children really did use it to explain their activities over the weekend to one another. Interestingly, I recently ran into Rufus, who is now a happy, healthy young man in his late teens. He no longer lives anywhere near Brony, and told me that, when he thinks of the village and the time he spent there growing up, it is that map he sees in his mind's eye. It came to symbolize his time at Little Scamps.

Many of the children I worked with in those days I never saw again. I would love to know what happened to Julie and Ross. I often think of Gus and his magic crayon, and hope the pair of them are doing well.

I did come across Mitzi several years later, although I scarcely recognized her. She was singing with a folk group at a concert to raise money for a local Irish language school, and was remarkably slim and lithe. She seemed to be well liked by her peers, and performed a solo that was heart-meltingly lovely.

Jeffrey left a year after I did to go on to a mainstream primary school where, with a classroom assistant to help him, he still struggled academically. His mother told me he was happy, though. I lost track of him after that.

Gilbert remained in special-care settings for the rest of his childhood, and is still in one, as far as I know. His particular difficulties made it impossible for him to adjust to life in 'normal' society. His parents employed an army of psychologists and therapists to try to 'cure' him, but to no avail.

Arga continued to have behavioural problems for several years, and remained at Little Scamps until she was eight, but eventually managed to make the transition to mainstream school. By then she was speaking English fluently and could read and write very well. She will be doing her Leaving Certificate this year.

Milandra left Little Scamps that September as planned, and excelled in her new school. Felicity and Tony were reunited and are still together. A teacher who had worked with Milandra informed me that she had rarely worked with a child who demonstrated such empathy with and compassion for others.

Dale and Kylie really did try to build a relationship with Tammy, and while the path was a rocky one, they made some progress. While Tammy never did go to a school for children with exceptional ability, she did go to one of the better local primaries, where a special subsidy helped pay for her books and other educational equipment. Sadly, Tammy was always attracted to trouble, and was excluded, then taken back but excluded again (this time for good) before she was twelve. I believe her educational career was patchy after that.

I heard from a social worker two years ago that she had come across Tammy in a unit for young offenders. She was involved in an educational programme there and was amazing her teachers. Unfortunately, she ran away consistently before they had a chance to get her through her exams. Some behaviours are very hard to change.

As I wrote of my friend Lonnie in *Little Boy Lost*, he died of a heart attack a year after the events of this book.

Tush was with him to the end.